Exploring the End Times

and

Interceding for Israel

Second Edition
Expanded and Updated

Rosamund Weissman

Exploring the End Times
and
Interceding for Israel

Second Edition
Expanded and Updated

Copyright © Rosamund Weissman 2021, 2023

Published by Fresh Olive Press
www.fresholivepress.com

ISBN 978-1-8382347-2-0
2nd edition 2023 (1st edition 2021)

Printed in the United Kingdom

Design and editing by Jonathan Weissman
Cover image by Lum3n sourced from pexels.com

Contents

O Come O Come Emmanuel

O come, O come, Emmanuel,
And ransom captive Israel,
That mourns in lonely exile here
Until the Son of God appear.
Rejoice! Rejoice! Emmanuel
Shall come to thee, O Israel.

O come, Thou Rod of Jesse, free
Thine own from Satan's tyranny;
From depths of hell Thy people save,
And give them victory o'er the grave.

O come, Thou dayspring, come and cheer
Our spirits by Thine advent here;
Disperse the gloomy clouds of night
And death's dark shadows put to flight!

O come, Thou Key of David, come,
And open wide our heavenly home;
Make safe the way that leads on high,
And close the path to misery.

O come, O come, Thou Lord of Might,
Who to Thy tribes on Sinai's height
In ancient times didst give the law
In cloud, and majesty, and awe.

Dedication and Thanks

This is dedicated to my lovely praying friend Sue, whose prayers have helped me on my way, and whose poetry can be found at my website **fresholivepress.com**. I am most grateful to the various Bible teachers whose ministries have guided my understanding. I have credited their material wherever possible throughout the text, and also in Further Resources. Finally, thank you to my husband Robert for your theological, historical and geographical editing, thank you to our son Jonathan for your hard work as editor and in designing the book cover, and thank you to our son Samuel for proofreading.

Note about Bible Translations

You may find it helpful when going through these studies to use more than one Bible. Some Bible translations seek to translate the Scriptures on a "word for word" basis, and others have a "thought for thought" approach. Both have their place and are useful. "Word for word" avoids the problem of a Bible translating team assuming something is figurative, whereas in fact it is literal. A "thought for thought" is helpful where certain Hebrew idioms, when translated literally, may cause confusion. Then, there are other Bibles that are paraphrases of the Scriptures, which will not be so useful for these studies.

לְמַעַן צִיּוֹן לֹא אֶחֱשֶׁה וּלְמַעַן
יְרוּשָׁלַם לֹא אֶשְׁקוֹט

l'ma-an tsion lo ekhesheh ool'ma-an

y'rooshalayim lo esh-kot

For Zion's sake I will not keep silent,

and for Jerusalem's sake I will not keep quiet.

Isaiah 62:1

Preface

Christians with a heart to pray for Israel may wonder what is ahead for the beloved nation, and how this may be reflected in their intercession. There will be readers who are particularly conscious of their role in teaching the next generation to navigate Biblical eschatology. Yet others will be seeking a springboard from which to launch into further personal or group Bible study. The writer of the book of Hebrews distinguishes between two sources of spiritual nourishment: milk and solid food. Various types of solid food require differing amounts of chewing. Tough cuts of meat can be hard work! Some of the topics ahead, such as on Daniel's 70-week prophecy and the statue in Nebuchadnezzar's dream, may require more chewing over, and so call for a second reading. The details supplied are important to grasp due to the role they play in the overall picture presented in this book. Interpretation of Biblical prophecy tends to be either literal or allegorical. Like most Jewish Christians, I hold to the former, and this leads me to a premillennial understanding, which you will find reflected in the pages within.

Testimony and Introduction

As a schoolgirl, who was growing up attending a Reform synagogue, my favourite hymn we sang in school assembly was *My eyes have seen the glory of the coming of the Lord.* I was totally ignorant of the meaning, particularly the part about the Lord trampling down the *grapes of wrath.* I did not have any Christian friends at school, with my impression of Christianity taken from a Church of England boarding school, Christ's Hospital, Hertford, which I attended for just over a year when I was 11. We had to go to chapel each weekday and on Sundays. I cannot recall ever hearing or being challenged by the gospel of salvation. Subsequently, in my teenage mind, Christianity had to be dull, boring and grey! However, some aspects of the faith jarred with this impression. In my A-level English Literature course, we studied the poem "The Second Coming" by W.B. Yeats. Our teacher told us that Christians believe Jesus will come again. I was astounded that the very people I assumed had such an insipid faith would be audacious enough to believe this! Additionally, I had the deepest of respect for Christians brave enough to go off to far-away lands as missionaries. Finally, I loved white church weddings which I saw on television! Immediately after completing my A levels, during the summer break, I had an intense desire to find God. I looked into Eastern religions like Hinduism and Buddhism and found them too complex to get my head around. I had a strong feeling that if God was knowable, then He would make it straightforward for us to understand the path to Him.

I spent much of my gap year in Israel as part of a Jewish young persons' programme based in Kibbutz Galed. This is a kibbutz on the Menashe Heights, which is a range running south-east from Mount Carmel parallel to the Jezreel Valley. It was only eight miles or so from Megiddo. I knew that the postal district was Megiddo, and like with the hymn at school, I had no idea of the eschatological significance. The scheme was called *Shnat Sherut*, meaning a *year of service*. The kibbutz had been founded in 1945 by German Zionists. The programme included working on the kibbutz and being taught the rudiments of the Hebrew language. The intention of those who ran the programme was to provide the youthful participants with a life-long connection to the Land.

As I stood ironing in the vast kibbutz laundry complex back in 1975, the ladies working around me were chattering away in German. I had never paid attention in German lessons at school, but if I had, perhaps I would have learned something of their story and how they arrived in Israel following the war. One of the first people I recall meeting out in the kibbutz pastures was a very cultured older German kibbutznik. He was interested to discover my name and where I was from. I told him my name was *Rosamund*, and, as we shook hands, he said *Ah, Schubert!* Being ignorant of the world of classical music, I thought that he was telling me that his name was Schubert, and it was some time before I realised that he was referring to the composer of the *Rosamunde Overture!*

Not all the members of the kibbutz were of German origin. I remember the head chef, who had terrible eyesight and thick glasses because, during the Holocaust, he had to be hidden in a cupboard in the Netherlands. Then there was Khava, the lady in charge of kitting out the volunteers. Khava greatly impressed me as she spoke many languages, including Hebrew, Swedish, Danish, and English. Her story was that, as a girl, she was part of the Jewish group smuggled out of Nazi-occupied Denmark to neutral Sweden. I also recall a flamboyant Spanish-speaking Kibbutznik working in the kitchen stirring delicious ratatouille in a huge open pot with one hand, and smoking her cigarette with the other. No one seemed too bothered where the ash fell! Back home, my friends did not generally take their Jewishness seriously. However, in Israel, among the other volunteers, for the first time I rubbed shoulders with fellow Jewish young people who let their faith affect their thinking and living, and they were more Orthodox in their outlook.

I returned from Israel with a love of the language and a determination to continue my search for God through my Jewishness. I went up a day late for my first term of university, as I decided for once to attend my home synagogue and fast on the Day of Atonement. The people in the synagogue were kind to one another about the challenge of fasting, but there was no talk nor sense of God being there. I was so disappointed not to find God on Yom Kippur, the holiest day of the Jewish calendar.

The following day when I arrived at university, I knocked on my neighbour's door in the hall of residence and sensed from looking around her room that she believed the Bible. I had the impression of Bibles, hymn books and even a Bible puzzle book. I had searched for God through Eastern religions and then through my Jewishness and wondered what kind of faith my neighbour had. So, I asked her if she was religious and the reply was that she would not say she was religious, but that she was a Christian. I then asked her what she believed. She told me that one day I would have to stand before God and give an account of everything I had ever done. I was absolutely stunned and felt convicted deep inside that I would not be able to argue my way out of this judgement as I used to attempt with my parents. As we spoke over the days, she challenged me to read the Old Testament for myself. What I did not know at the time was that this faithful young woman had spent the summer vacation reading through the Old Testament and praying for the person she would be living next door to at university!

I was jealous that my new friend knew the Jewish Scriptures so much better than I did! I was deeply struck in my readings by the verses which predicted the regathering of the Jewish people to the Land of Israel, because I had so recently been there among Jews from many nations. Another verse that really hit home to me was Isaiah 29:13, which says "Because this people draw near with their words and honor Me with their lip service, but they remove their hearts far from Me and their reverence for Me consists of tradition learned by rote." This struck me deeply as being exactly what I had just observed in the synagogue for myself.

I was fascinated by prophetic passages as they related to the Messiah such as Isaiah 53:5, Jeremiah 31:31-34, Micah 5:2 and Zechariah 13:1. My friend passed on to me a Bible study presenting the Gospel using entirely Old Testament verses, and I could see that there was not a soul who did not sin, and I read about God providing a fountain for sin and uncleanness. When I finally took the plunge and opened the first book of the New Testament and started to read the genealogy of the Lord Jesus in Matthew's Gospel, I just knew that this New Covenant was for Jewish people. A little later, I read in the book of Romans that a true Jew was one whose heart was circumcised. It made sense to me. My friend invited me to attend *All Souls, Langham Place* in December 1976. She was very struck by the appropriateness of the hymn that was sung that day, *O Come, O Come Emmanuel.* I prayed there to receive the Lord Jesus as my personal Saviour. You may find the lyrics of that Advent hymn particularly moving in light of the subject matter of this book. Soon after praying, I had these words ringing in my ears, which I had not realised that I knew: *Because you have done this thing, and not withheld your son, your only son.* Whilst I did not completely understand its meaning at the time, it brought to mind Abraham sacrificing Isaac, a wonderful bridge between my Jewish heritage and my subsequent trust in the Messiah of Israel.

My family was appalled to hear of my decision, and my late grandfather refused to have me in his house for some years. My grandmother hoped to save me from my supposed error and took me to an Orthodox rabbi in the hope that he would talk me out of this faith. I felt so embarrassed for my grandmother, because when she took me into his Jewish centre of learning, he would have nothing to do with us because we were women!

Sadly, this grandmother became very hard against the Lord, as my husband patiently and faithfully shared the Gospel with her over the years. Sometimes she would say that we were mad to believe in Jesus, and at other times she would tell Robert that he was too clever for her! Almost the last thing she told my husband and myself was that if she lived to be a thousand, she would never believe in Jesus. When she passed away, I was given a message that my husband was banned from her funeral. This was because of his work as an evangelist to the Jews. I felt that I too could not attend her funeral, out of loyalty to my husband, so I never got to say the final farewell to this grandmother whom I loved dearly, and who showed many kindnesses to our family as we were raising our three sons. She used to be very mocking of the ultra-Orthodox in London and called them *cowboys* because of their strange hats. Ironically, a cousin on that side of the family, one of her grandsons, subsequently moved to Jerusalem, where he is now one of the ultra-Orthodox with a large family. He may have been sent to a Jewish school as a reaction to my accepting Yeshua as my Saviour.

One of the first things I did as a new Jewish believer in Yeshua was to return to Israel for six weeks during the following summer vacation to work on a different kibbutz. The Lord led me to Kibbutz Reshafim, where two Christian volunteers from Canada had been praying for the Lord to send a Jewish believer to them to show the people on the kibbutz that Jewish people can believe in Jesus. This kibbutz was near the base of Mount Gilboa, which is on the south-east side of the Jezreel Valley, the site of the final defeat of King Saul and his son Jonathan. It was a short walk over the fields to catch the bus from Beit She'an. Those of us staying on the kibbutz thought very little of walking among the city's rich tapestry of partially unearthed Roman and Byzantine remains, such as the amphitheatre and various ancient statues. This time I had a little more Biblical understanding of my location! I was much later to learn that both Kibbutz Galed and Kibbutz Reshafim are located within the boundaries of the land granted to the tribe of Manasseh.[1] It is certainly a fertile land. I have memories of picking oranges in the orchard, being told I could eat as many as I wanted, and soon getting fed up with the taste!

A year or so later, my new friend at university who was by then discipling me, suggested I memorise Isaiah Chapter 40

[1] Joshua 17:11; Judges 1:27

during one of my vacations. This was a challenge I willingly accepted. However, some 45 years later, in writing the second edition of this book, the Lord has finally shown me a deeper meaning to this precious chapter. These insights are set out at the end of this book in "Thoughts on Isaiah 40," best read after the main chapters.

After Robert called on my other grandmother as part of his evangelistic outreach in the East End of London, she introduced us to each other. Robert has been an evangelist to Jewish people and a Bible teacher since 1975, and refers to me as his reward for evangelism! The first sermon I heard my husband-to-be preach in 1983 was on the prophetic statue in Daniel 2. During subsequent years as a Jewish believer in the Lord Jesus, I have had a keen interest in the End Times, modern Hebrew, and a great love for Israel. My understanding of eschatology has gradually developed and changed over the decades. I have enjoyed leading many ladies' Bible studies in churches, often on the prophetic Scriptures and the End Times, learning more modern Hebrew, and teaching beginners' Hebrew to adults. I read and listened to many Bible teachers. These helpful teachings were usually focused on the book of Revelation. I learned about how a European Antichrist would unite all the nations to follow a one-world religion, which he would head up, and I used to wonder, *what about the Muslims, would they abandon their faith to join this new one-world religion?* I read in the Old Testament about how Israel would be regathered to honour the Lord their God in holiness, and I had to admit that Israel was certainly not yet honouring the Lord.

In recent years, the final parts of the puzzle started coming together for me. I am now seeking to help readers understand the End Times further, and to be equipped to pray accordingly. The first part of this book will mainly focus on the place of Israel in the End Times. Then we will move on to survey our subject through a wider lens, keeping Israel firmly in our sights.

1: The Prayer Wall

"On your walls, O Jerusalem, I have appointed watchmen; all day and all night they will never keep silent. You who remind the LORD, take no rest for yourselves; and give Him no rest until He establishes and makes Jerusalem a praise in the earth." (Isaiah 62:6-7)

There are many Christians praying for Israel today, and yet there is a gap in the wall of prayer, concerning Israel at the end of the age. One of the key purposes of this book is to help to bridge this gap. God is seeking intercessors whose hearts resonate with His. He is looking for individuals to understand, and be moved by, the significance of what is coming upon this world. Isaiah tells us, "And He saw that there was no man, and was astonished that there was no one to intercede."[2]

The Lord is looking for those who never tire of bringing their cause to Him, like the importunate widow.[3] Are we among those whom He is calling to the task of watching and praying? This is a ministry which God highly values. In the time of Ezekiel, the future of the city of Jerusalem hung in the divine balance, "I searched for a man among them who would build up the wall and stand in the gap before Me for the land, so that I would not destroy it; but I found no one."[4] As a result of there being no intercessor, the Babylonians destroyed the city in 586 BC. God said, "thus I have poured out My indignation on them."

During Nehemiah's service as governor of Jerusalem, he led the project to rebuild the walls of the city which had previously been destroyed by the Babylonians. Three days after

---

[2] Isaiah 59:16
[3] Luke 18:1-8
[4] Ezekiel 22:30

arriving, Nehemiah secretly surveyed the walls under the cover of night. When he realised how rundown they were, he rallied Judah's leaders to undertake the rebuilding project. The enemies of Judah laughed when hearing of his plan.[5] Nehemiah realised that any gaps in the wall would enable the enemy to easily infiltrate and wreak havoc upon the restored city and temple.

Now that Israel is approaching her end-times testing, intercessors can likewise be said to form a wall of protection around Israel, standing between the nation and her enemies. The builders in the time of Nehemiah worked wearing swords, as the trumpeter readied to sound the alarm nearby.[6] As watchmen, we likewise need to avail ourselves of the sword of the Spirit and to sound the alarm (blow the trumpet)[7] to recruit like-minded Christians to join with us in prayer, offering ourselves as *living stones* in this wall.[8]

Nehemiah divided the task of rebuilding the walls into manageable sections. The people worked willingly and methodically, keeping watch for the enemy and co-operating with one another. Each of the twelve gates was repaired.[9] Individual households repaired different sections, some of which were near to, or opposite, their homes. The priests repaired the Sheep Gate through which the animals were brought for the temple sacrifices. Everyone worked on the part of the project that was appropriate for them.

---

[5] Nehemiah 2:12-19, 4:1-3
[6] Nehemiah 4:18, subsequently half worked and half bore weapons (4:21)
[7] Joel 2:1; Jeremiah 4:5,19; Hosea 5:8; 8:1; Jeremiah 6:17; Ezekiel 33:3-6
[8] 1 Peter 4:4-5
[9] Nehemiah 3, 12:39

We likewise need not be overwhelmed by the magnitude of the task to pray for Israel in the End Times. We need to see ourselves simply as one individual in the church's collective *prayer wall*. We should pray in accordance with the burden the Lord lays upon our hearts. When each of us occupy our strategic position in prayer, then the wall is complete. Just as the enemies of Judah grew very angry as they saw the closing up of the gaps in the walls of Jerusalem,[10] so our prayers will disturb the spiritual powers of wickedness already set against Israel. The enemy will have many strategies to breach the *wall of prayer* around Jerusalem and Israel.[11] However, "we are not ignorant of his schemes."[12] "Therefore, my beloved brethren, be steadfast, immovable, always abounding in the work of the Lord, knowing that your toil is not in vain in the Lord."[13] We will make a difference through our intercession.

We need as intercessors to bear in mind certain distinctives in praying for Israel. Israel is spoken of in the verse "but to this day whenever Moses is read, a veil lies over their hearts."[14] Again, Israel is referred to in the Scripture, "a partial hardening has happened to Israel until the fullness of the Gentiles has come in."[15] It is essential that we pray within the revealed will of God as outlined in the Bible. The veil will only be lifted from the heart of the remnant of the nation when national salvation comes to Israel, as will be discussed later in this book. The Lord speaks of that event when He says, "I will give them one heart, and put a new spirit within them. And I will remove

---

[10] Nehemiah 4:7
[11] Isaiah 7:6
[12] 2 Corinthians 2:11
[13] 1 Corinthians 15:58
[14] 2 Corinthians 3:15
[15] Romans 11:25

the heart of stone from their flesh and give them a heart of flesh."[16] For now, we need to be praying for the lifting of the veil in the softened hearts of individual Jewish people, rather than for the nation as a whole. It is mainly religious Jewish men who read the five books of Moses, and indeed they need the veil lifting. For the majority of Jewish people, it is the hardness of heart (translated as "blindness" in some Bibles) we need to be praying about. This blindness manifests itself in many ways similar to the Gentile world. Jewish people can be very committed to materialism, Darwinism, and socialising at events such as Bar Mitzvahs, weddings, and celebrations such as circumcisions and Purim.

We are given another clue about how to pray when we are instructed concerning unsaved Jewish people, "they did not stumble so as to fall, did they? Far from it! But by their wrongdoing salvation *has come* to the Gentiles, to make them jealous."[17] Both my husband and I were individually provoked to put our faith in Jesus after we were each made jealous by the faith of the fellow student who witnessed to us in our respective universities. So we can be praying for individual Jewish people to encounter Christians directly, or through the media, who one way or another cause them to be jealous of their faith.

A further distinctive in praying for Jewish people is the matter of the trauma from the Holocaust, the horror of which continues to reverberate down through the generations. Those directly brought up by Holocaust survivors will inevitably be emotionally disturbed or scarred. I heard one lady explain that when she had problems at school, her mother, a Holocaust survivor, would say to her that at least she had a school to go

---

[16] Ezekiel 11:19
[17] Romans 11:11

to, and then would switch off emotionally, leaving her daughter unsupported. It does not take much imagination to picture the struggles that daughter would have faced bringing up her own family. Even reading about people's experiences in the Holocaust can be extremely disturbing to sensitive Jewish people. As Israel faces and goes through the *Time of Jacob's Trouble*, the tendency will be for this trauma to be stirred up in those who need to know the ever-deepening presence of the Prince of Peace.

I recently asked a Messianic leader in the land of Israel what sort of issues we should pray about. He replied that he values our prayers to see: the kingdom of Yeshua advance, the unity of believers, the salvation of Israel, general revival in the land, repentance, holiness, and the refining of the saints. Many of us are already strengthening Israel by faithfully praying along these lines. I know that this leader believes in the coming time of testing ahead for the nation, yet he did not mention it. This is the gap in the wall of prayer in which the readers of this book are invited to stand and co-labour.

Why does God look for intercessors when He acts as He wills anyway? One answer is that He delights to work with us as part of His relationship with us.[18] As labourers in the church, we are "God's fellow workers."[19] As we spend time with the Lord, praying about matters which are so close to His heart, we may find our own emotional response to what is ahead starts to reflect, in some degree, how God feels. We may find ourselves sharing a measure of His eventual joy. Just as the farmer rejoices at finding his one lost sheep out of 100, so

---

[18] Mark 16:20; John 15:15
[19] 1 Corinthians 3:9

too the angels rejoice over just one sinner repenting.[20] Based on this alone, the Lord's joy in the eventual national salvation of surviving Israel will be immeasurable. "He will exult over you with joy, He will be quiet in His love, He will rejoice over you with shouts of joy."[21]

We will not only share in the Lord's joy but also in His heavy heart concerning what is ahead. This aspect of His character is revealed by Isaiah who wrote about the approaching judgement coming upon the cities of ancient Moab. He reflected the heavy heart of God when he spoke of weeping bitter tears, saying, "I will drench you with my tears."[22] In the New Testament, we see that Jesus wept as He approached Jerusalem, because He knew what was to come upon the city and its people.[23] "Jerusalem, Jerusalem, who kills the prophets and stones those who are sent to her! How often I wanted to gather your children together, the way a hen gathers her chicks under her wings."[24]

Daniel fasted as he sought the LORD, humbling himself and confessing both his personal sin and the sin of his people.[25] Jeremiah was known as the *weeping prophet*, because he was so devastated by the suffering of his people that he could reflect, "O that my head were waters, and my eyes a fountain of tears, that I might weep day and night for the slain of the daughter of my people."[26] Looking ahead to the *Time of Jacob's Trouble*, we too may weep for Israel's tribulation to come, and

---

[20] Luke 15:1-7
[21] Zephaniah 3:17
[22] Isaiah 16:9
[23] Luke 19:41-44
[24] Matthew 23:37
[25] Daniel 9:3-4, 20-23
[26] Jeremiah 9:1

for those Jewish souls separated from the presence of Lord forever. May our hearts beat with God's, as we weep and cry out with passion, "Spare Your people O LORD."[27]

May all who love Israel pray and fast with the commitment of Queen Esther, "For how can I endure to see the calamity which will befall my people." Indeed, as was the case for Esther, we too may have come to the Kingdom "for such a time as this."[28] When we fast, we make ourselves weak, and yet this brings the strength of Almighty God into our prayer lives. The Apostle Paul boasted of his weaknesses so that the power (*dunamis*, related to the English words for dynamite and dynamic) of the Lord Jesus would be his. He said, "for when I am weak, then I am strong."[29] Let us pray for the Lord to raise up more *Esthers* to bless Israel by labouring in prayer and fasting. Pray too for completion of the wall of prayer around her.

In those times when our hearts are heavy, or we just do not know what to pray for, the Spirit "intercedes for us with groanings too deep for words."[30] We too may find ourselves groaning in prayer at times. The Lord Jesus prayed "with loud crying and tears."[31] Bitter *tears* formed the prayer of King Hezekiah and God duly granted him another 15 years of life in response.[32] We too can offer our tears to the Lord as our prayer. If you find that deep feelings are stirred in your heart as you read this book, it may be helpful to express them in

---

[27] Joel 2:17
[28] Esther 4:14-16, 8:6
[29] 2 Corinthians 12:9-10
[30] Romans 8:26-27
[31] Hebrews 5:7
[32] Isaiah 38:3

some creative manner. You can read my personal musings in the Epilogue.

The Apostle Paul describes Gentiles as being privileged debtors to the Jewish people, even going as far as to say, "if the Gentiles have shared in their spiritual things, they are indebted to minister to them also in material things."[33] The context is that of Gentile believers in the early church providing financial help for impoverished Jewish believers in Jerusalem. How much more does the church today have a duty to minister to the Jewish people in intercession, especially as believers become aware of the impending *Time of Jacob's Trouble*?

Let us say with the Psalmist, "Peace be upon Israel."[34] May we also confidently look forward to our reward, "Your watchmen lift up their voices, they shout joyfully together; for they will see with their own eyes when the LORD restores Zion."[35]

Israel	יִשְׂרָאֵל

[33] Romans 15:27
[34] Psalm 125:5
[35] Isaiah 52:8

2: Jacob's Troubles

"For thus says the LORD, 'I have heard a sound of terror, of dread, and there is no peace. Ask now, and see if a male can give birth. Why do I see every man with his hands on his loins, as a woman in childbirth? And why have all faces turned pale? Alas! for that day is great, there is none like it; and it is the time of Jacob's distress, but he will be saved from it." (Jeremiah 30:5-7)

This passage refers to Jacob's distress, also known as the *Time of Jacob's Trouble*, which is one of the terms for the final three and a half years of this age. Other names for this period include the *Great Tribulation*. Sadly, over the course of history, Jacob's people have suffered various troubles or distresses, some of which we will consider in this chapter.

In the book of Genesis, we read how, after Jacob wrestled with the Lord, God renamed him *Israel*.[36] The meaning of this new name is one who fights victoriously with God. The last two letters of his new name, *el*, is Hebrew for God. When we feel burdened to pray for Israel, but do not know how to pray, we can appeal to God on the grounds that the nation bears His name. We can echo the sentiment of Jeremiah who said, "we are called by Your name; do not forsake us!"[37]

We see both names concurrently in the Bible, such as when "God spoke to Israel in visions of the night and said, 'Jacob, Jacob."[38] So, when we are talking about *Jacob's trouble*, this is a reference to Israel's affliction. The twelve tribes of Israel descend from Jacob's twelve sons. Scripture shows us the value God places upon Jacob's family. Outstandingly, and

---

[36] Genesis 32:24-28
[37] Jeremiah 14:9
[38] Genesis 46:2

of special significance to Jews and Christians, is the faith of Jacob's grandfather Abraham, who was willing to offer his son Isaac on the altar to the LORD. We see the value Jacob places on his prophetic birthright compared to the attitude of Esau, and read of God's perspective on the situation, how He loved Jacob and hated Esau.[39] We learn from the New Testament that the whole family of Israel is beloved for the sake of the patriarchs (Abraham, Isaac and Jacob).[40] We are told that in the New Jerusalem the names of the twelve tribes will be written on the gates.[41] In the New Testament, we are still reminded about the tribal divisions, like where we read of Anna, the prophetess from the tribe of Asher.[42] The Apostle Paul tells us twice that he was from the tribe of Benjamin.[43]

God chose to make a solemn covenant with the patriarchs of Israel. The Abrahamic covenant is set out in the book of Genesis, which includes the words, "I will make you a great nation, and I will bless you, and make your name great; and so you shall be a blessing."[44] Part of this promise includes the land of Israel, with designated boundaries, as described in the book of Genesis.[45] God passed the covenant from Abraham to Isaac,[46] and then from Isaac to Jacob.[47] The whole issue of the physical land of Israel is so important that the book of Ezekiel details the future allocated borders of the land and the tribal

---

[39] Genesis 25:29-34; Malachi 1:2-3
[40] Romans 11:28
[41] Revelation 21:12
[42] Luke 2:36
[43] Romans 11:1; Philippians 3:5
[44] Genesis 12:1-3
[45] Genesis 15:18-21
[46] Genesis 13:15, 26:2-5
[47] Genesis 28:12-15

divisions after the Second Coming.[48] Understanding the promise of the Land of Israel to the people of Jacob is fundamental to comprehending the End Times.

The context of the phrase, the *Time of Jacob's Trouble*, is instructive.[49] We read there that the prophet asks why he sees every man with a pale face, looking like a woman in labour. Jeremiah goes on to say that Jacob will be delivered from the time of his distress. The prophet Daniel speaks of that time in these terms: "And there will be a time of distress such as never occurred since there was a nation until that time."[50] Jesus tells us "for then there will be a great tribulation, such as has not occurred since the beginning of the world until now, nor ever will."[51] It is sobering to think about these descriptions of the future suffering of Jacob's people.

However painful we may find this to be, we cannot absorb the magnitude of what is ahead for Israel, without considering her past and present suffering. We need this comparison because the future *Time of Jacob's Trouble* will be worse than anything that went before, and nothing will ever subsequently equal it.

Israel has had many severe afflictions in her history such as the Assyrian and Babylonian invasions during Old Testament times.[52] We have some figures for the later Jewish-Roman wars, when Josephus[53] estimated that during the siege of Jerusalem in AD 70, over a million civilians died in the city.

---

[48] Ezekiel 47:13 to 48:8
[49] Jeremiah 30:5-9
[50] Daniel 12:1
[51] Matthew 24:21
[52] For dates, see Chart of Chronology of Relevant History on page 154
[53] A Jewish contemporary historian from a priestly family, who served in the Roman empire

Josephus also wrote that 97,000 were taken away as slaves at that time.

We read in Hosea 9:17 that the Jews will be wanderers among the nations, and sadly we have seen this being played out over the centuries. The Jewish people have been expelled from dozens of countries. Their history in England is most sobering. Medieval church law forbade the lending of money with interest by Christians, and left this role to the Jews. They were hated as *Christ killers,* and even accused of murdering children to use their blood as an ingredient in the unleavened bread, *matzah,* eaten at Passover. That claim was particularly offensive bearing in mind the prohibition of the consumption of blood in Leviticus 17:10-14.

The first European country to expel Jews was England. This occurred in 1290, at the hand of Edward I. One hundred years earlier, about 150 Jewish people lost their lives in the castle of York, entrapped by their persecutors. We read in 1 Kings 9:7 how Israel will be cut off from their land, and so "Israel will become a proverb and a byword among all peoples." In Pakistan, for example, the word for Jew, *Yahudi*, is used as an insult, which must bring sadness to the heart of the Lord.

The Holocaust is fresh in our minds. I mentioned Khava in my testimony, the lady on the kibbutz originally from Denmark. The Danish government refused to co-operate with the Germans when they were invaded. By the time the Germans were ready to round up the Jewish population en-route to the concentration camps, the Danish government had organised hiding places for most of the Jewish people in Copenhagen, and entered into an agreement with Sweden to shelter them. A journey was organised, rather like the British rescue of the armed forces from the beaches of Dunkirk during World War II, using small private and fishing boats. Thus, the lives of 90% of the Jewish population of Denmark were saved, and so Khava survived. Jewish deaths in Denmark were in the region of 100. Contrast that to a nation like Ukraine, with large numbers of the population who were anti-Semitic. It is thought that the Ukrainian authorities helped round up Jewish people for mass killings. The number killed may have been 1.5 million, about 70% of the Jewish population. We will see in a later chapter how it very much matters to the Lord how the nations treat His beloved ancient people.

Since the future *Time of Jacob's Trouble* will be unequalled by anything that preceded it, the Holocaust needs also to be considered in terms of the overall number who tragically perished. Hitler is estimated to have murdered six million Jews in the Shoah (Holocaust).[54] The true number may well be much higher.

As of December 2022, the State of Israel has a population of just over nine and a half million, which is expected to rise to more than 10 million in the following five years.[55] Almost 74% of Israel's current population (about 7 million) is Jewish.[56] The population of Jerusalem in 2022 was over 950,000, over 60% of whom are Jewish.[57] The number of Jewish people living outside Israel is thought to be approximately eight million.[58] This area of dispersion from the land of Israel is known

---

[54] The word *Shoah* is the Hebrew word for destruction, *Holocaust* is the Greek word for a burnt offering made to God

[55] "Israel: Total population from 2017 to 2027", www.statista.com, accessed February 2023

[56] www.jewishvirtuallibray.org, accessed February 2023

[57] www.worldpopulationreview.com, accessed February 2023

[58] www.jewishagency.org, accessed February 2023

as the *diaspora*. It has been said that hardly any Jewish people live in the same land as their grandfather was born. In my family, it was my great-grandparents' generation which struggled with English. They came from Lithuania and Latvia. My husband's grandfathers were born in Kiev (currently in Ukraine) and Poland.

The subject of violent anti-Semitism is not confined to history and prophetic books. The incessant anti-Semitism in modern-day France from political and religious extremists is a painful subject. We read media reports of murderous attacks, desecration of gravestones, Jewish children being withdrawn from mainstream schools for their own safety, and mass emigration to Israel and elsewhere. The heart-breaking attack in Paris on a kosher supermarket in January 2015 is of relevance to our subject matter. The attacker claimed to be a member of the Islamic State. Four brave Jewish men were murdered, ranging in age from early 20s to mid-60s. It was followed by a knife attack on a Jewish teacher in 2016 in Marseille. The boy who carried out this stabbing was said to have been inspired by Islamic State.

Subsequently, the debate started in France as to whether Jewish men should cease wearing their *yarmulkes* (head coverings) in public, as suggested by a Jewish leader in Marseille. The number of Jewish people living in France is sizeable, exceeded only by the Jewish populations of Israel and the United States. Many Jewish people in France no longer feel safe. France is a secular country and claims not to wish to be seen as interfering in religious matters. Perhaps some intercessors will feel a particular burden for the Jews of France. They need wisdom as to their future, daily protection, and a supportive government. Many are moving to Israel, spurred on by the tragic events in 2015. These French Jews feel vulnerable and unprotected in France and seek the relative security of living in Israel, where they anticipate a brighter future for their children. Pray too for those labouring in France to reach the Jewish community with the gospel.

We need to be praying for our local Jewish community here in the United Kingdom and Republic of Ireland. Remember the evangelists and churches reaching out to them. Much of the U.K.'s Jewish population of nearly 300,000 live in Greater London and nearby counties. There are 28,000 in the Manchester conurbation, 6,000 in Leeds, 2,000 in Brighton, a mere 900 in both Glasgow and Edinburgh, and only 300 live in Belfast. The Republic of Ireland is said to have about 2,600 Jewish people, two-thirds living in Dublin.[59]

We would all like to think that the Holocaust was that terrible final time of suffering, but we always need to look at context when considering Scripture. Jeremiah tells us of great things the Lord will do to rescue Israel *on that day*.[60] He will set the Jewish people free from their servitude to foreigners and, instead of serving those people, we read in the passage: "they shall serve the LORD their God and David their king, whom I will raise up for them." This physical liberation and spiritual revival have not yet happened, so we must reluctantly conclude that the ultimate *Time of Jacob's Trouble* is yet to come.

In Daniel 12:1-3, we see how the trouble is placed in an eschatological (End Times) context, as it speaks of "many of those who sleep in the dust of the ground will awake, these to

---

59 www.jewishvirtuallibrary.org
60 Jeremiah 30:8-11

everlasting life, but the others to disgrace and everlasting contempt." Again, this has not yet happened. There was no resurrection of the dead for reward or punishment following the Holocaust. Finally, turning to Matthew 24:15-31, we see that this is unarguably set in the End Times, just as Jesus is about to return. Nothing that has happened so far in Jerusalem has been accompanied by the sort of signs that Jesus describes in this passage, such as the stars falling from heaven. We read "they will see the SON OF MAN COMING ON THE CLOUDS OF THE SKY with power and great glory."[61]

This context is so important, because some Christians do not accept the thought of yet more suffering for Israel, the apple of God's eye. These sincere brethren understandably will contend that the ultimate *Time of Jacob's Trouble* was the horrendous treatment of the Jews by Nazi Germany, and that the Bible's promises of regathering, and of a wonderful future, were fulfilled by the birth of the State of Israel in 1948. Looking at the context as we have just done, it is not realistic to say that the prophecies in Jeremiah, Daniel and Matthew were completely fulfilled by the tragic event of the Holocaust and the re-establishment of the modern State of Israel. 1948 was undoubtedly of huge prophetic significance but was merely the beginning of the revival of the dried bones in the valley, spoken of in Ezekiel 37:1-14.

| unleavened bread | *matzah* | מַצָּה |

3: The Temple

"Therefore when you see the ABOMINATION OF DESOLATION which was spoken of through Daniel the prophet, standing in the holy place (let the reader understand), then those who are in Judea must flee to the mountains." (Matthew 24:15-16)

As we examine the role of Israel in the End Times, we are focusing on the future temple to be built in Jerusalem. God tells us that He has placed the city of Jerusalem in the centre of the nations.[62] Just as the Bible centres on Israel, the city of Jerusalem and specifically on the temple, so our watchfulness is helpfully directed first to the temple site, then to the city of Jerusalem, then to the land of Israel, and then to the Jewish people dispersed across the world. This reflects Jesus' instruction to the apostles "you shall be My witnesses, both in Jerusalem, and in all Judea and Samaria, and even to the remotest part of the earth."[63]

Herod's Temple was much admired in the time of Jesus, comprised of wonderful buildings adorned with lovely stones and decorative offerings.[64] Jesus explained to His disciples that the temple would be destroyed stone by stone.[65] The disciples asked when these things will happen. It is a very fair question, and one which Jesus took time to answer in Matthew 24-25, a passage known as the *Olivet Discourse*. It is given this name because Jesus was speaking on the Mount of Olives, which is to the east of Jerusalem and overlooks the temple area. The very fact that Jesus supplies such extensive details about the End Times is an indication of the importance of our subject. We

---

[62] Ezekiel 5:5
[63] Acts 1:8
[64] Luke 21:5
[65] Matthew 24:2-3

know that the Romans destroyed Herod's temple and left Jerusalem desolate in AD 70, but the Jewish people neither called out for their Messiah nor cried, "BLESSED IS HE WHO COMES IN THE NAME OF THE LORD."[66] This tells us that there will yet be a further fulfilment of His prophecy.

The warning by Jesus to his disciples to flee to the mountains was initially heeded by the Jewish Christians escaping from Jerusalem during the time of the Roman campaign to besiege the city. They fled to the wilderness city of Pella on the eastern side of the River Jordan, thereby saving their lives. This was an early parting of the ways between the Messianic section of the Jewish community in Jerusalem and those who stayed behind. The second fulfilment will yet dramatically take place in the End Times when Messianic Jews flee Jerusalem at the time the Antichrist desecrates the future temple.

Jesus combined both events in His instructions in the Olivet Discourse. How fitting that the Lord was looking down at the temple as He delivered this monumental message about His Second Coming! Since there is currently no temple in Jerusalem, the fact that the Bible predicts an end-times desecration tells us that the temple will be rebuilt. This will be the third temple, sometimes referred to as the *Tribulation Temple*, and it will be the focal point of events in the End Times. The prophet Daniel describes the pivotal moment that will usher in the *Time of Jacob's Trouble*. He writes of the future Antichrist ending the sacrifices and offerings made in the temple and putting in it the *abomination of desolation*.[67] This describes something outrageously sacrilegious being placed in the temple.

---

[66] Matthew 23:39
[67] Daniel 11:31

The future temple will follow the pattern of the earlier temples. There will be an altar for the Levitical priests to sacrifice animals as burnt offerings and peace offerings, following the instructions in Exodus 20:24. Hebrews 9:1-5 provides us with details of the various temple furnishings and items which will need to be constructed and gathered in the rebuilt temple. Listed there are such items as the lampstand, the table with the 12 special loaves of bread on it, the gold altar of incense and the gold-covered Ark of the Covenant. It is hard for us to imagine temple sacrifices restarting in the future, as in Old Testament times, yet this has always been the main function of the temple building.

The Temple Institute in Jerusalem has already made the items of temple furnishings in readiness, and is training priests to minister there. They understand that the current state of rabbinical Judaism is a very poor reflection of the Biblical instructions for Israelite religious life given to Moses in the Torah (the first five books of the Old Testament). It is from among the ranks of the Ultra-Orthodox (*Haredim* or trembling ones) that this yearning arises for the temple to be rebuilt.

These requirements include the observance of the weekly Sabbath. Numbers 28:9-10 institutes offerings for the Sabbath: two lambs with fine flour and oil. This an impossible requirement today for the Ultra-Orthodox, who seek to honour the Sabbath as laid out in the Law of Moses. They attend synagogue, rest from work, dine as a family and recite various blessings. Yet they are not able to make the prescribed temple offerings. Rabbinic Judaism, which has developed since the destruction of the temple in AD 70, is very different to the Biblical Old Testament model. It is an attempt to continue Jewish life without the temple sacrifices.

After the destruction of Herod's Temple, a group of rabbis met in Yavneh, on the coast of Israel. Their task was to find the way forward for Judaism without the temple. There could be no more temple sacrifices. The role of these offerings was to instruct Israel as to the need for the innocent to die on behalf of the sinner. The rabbis decided that prayer would take the place of sacrifices. The synagogue would have to completely replace the temple, rather than function in addition to it. The rabbis thus put the people on the path of working to prove how morally good they are, establishing their own righteousness, as described by the Apostle Paul.[68] Devout Jewish people, like many other religious followers, seek opportunities to do good works (in Hebrew *mitzvot*).

It is hard for Christians to understand the depths of outrage that will be felt by the Orthodox over the future desecration of the rebuilt temple. The Antichrist will be showing utter contempt for the God of Israel and revealing his satanic desire to receive the worship of man, declaring that this is the place for that adoration. The Apostle Paul tells us the Antichrist will be one who "opposes and exalts himself above every so-called god or object of worship, so that he takes his seat in the temple of God, displaying himself as being God."[69]

Those evangelical Christians who witness the establishment and operation of the Tribulation temple will have different opinions. Some will view it as an affront to the finished sacrificial work of the Lord Jesus, whilst others will point out that Paul refers to it as the "temple of God." For now, we can all at least respect that the Temple Institute's plans are tacit

---

[68] Romans 10:3
[69] 2 Thessalonians 2:4

acknowledgment that bloodless Judaism is fundamentally inadequate.

Is there time to build a solid structure (complete with foundations) before the Temple's prophesied desecration? We should bear in mind that architectural plans for the third temple have already been prepared, and that Herod only took 18 months to renovate the sanctuary of the second temple.[70] Additionally, it could be desecrated as early as its first week of service. Lastly, the temple furniture could initially be set up in a specially designed marquee (or similar temporary structure) akin to the Old Testament tabernacle.

The Ultra-Orthodox learn in religious centres,[71] where most of their time is spent studying rabbinic commentaries known as the Talmud,[72] rather than the Old Testament. Parts of these rabbinic writings disparage the Lord Jesus, even claiming He deserved death for practicing sorcery and for provoking Israel to idolatry.[73] This often further entrenches any pre-existing Jewish hostility towards faith in Jesus as Messiah.

By contrast, the reinstatement of the temple will represent a partial return to Biblical practices. Unlike Talmudic traditions, this will bring to life Old Testament verses like, "For the life of the flesh is in the blood, and I have given it to you on the altar to make atonement for your souls; for it is the blood by reason of the life that makes atonement."[74]

---

[70] Israel My Glory internet article, "The Lord's Temple in Jerusalem."
[71] "yeshivot." Singular "yeshivah"
[72] The Talmud was written in and edited between the 3rd and 6th centuries, languages used Hebrew and Aramaic (Chabad.org What is the Talmud? Definition and Comprehensive Guide)
[73] Sanhedrin 43a,107, Gittin 56b and 57a, Berachot 17b
[74] Leviticus 17:11

The temple's desecration at the hands of the Antichrist will betray Israel's trust, taking place halfway through the final seven years of this age. Many prophecy teachers expect this period to coincide with a seven-year peace agreement between Israel and her enemies. We will look at this in more detail later. But for now, bear in mind that any such agreement will likely yet include the right for the Jewish people to rebuild the temple on the Temple Mount site. This future *abomination of desolation* will be the Antichrist's declaration of war on all that Israel holds dear – peace, security and temple sacrifices.

Jesus makes a point to express practical concern for those days and to emphasise the urgency of the flight from Jerusalem.[75] He says, for example, "whoever is on the housetop must not go down to get the things out that are in his house. Whoever is in the field must not turn back to get his cloak." We may want to express some of Jesus' words in language that we can relate to better, perhaps seeing those *out in the field* as including those out at work. We should pray that, as the peace agreement unfolds in the early months and years, what is ahead will become even more obvious to the believers in the land at that time. We may wish to pray that they will warn their fellow countrymen ahead of the event. Israel is notorious for not listening to its prophets, particularly paying no regard to what Jesus says, "Jerusalem, Jerusalem who kills the prophets and stones those who are sent to her."[76]

The *Haredim* form about one-third of the Jewish population of Jerusalem, the remaining Jewish people being either less strictly devoted to Judaism or secular. As we pray for Israel in the End Times, it is helpful to understand a little of the

---

[75] Matthew 24:15-22
[76] Matthew 23:37

mindset of the ultra-Orthodox who have large families, averaging seven children. They seek to fulfil the commandment, "Be fruitful and multiply."[77] Their young couples also delight in being able to bring children into the world to play their part in rebuilding the Jewish population after Hitler's devastation during the Holocaust. Contraception is officially permitted only in very limited circumstances, such as after a Caesarean delivery, or for the purpose of spacing the children. This in turn suggests that we should pray for the many parents and young children who will be caught up in the horrors yet to come to Jerusalem.

We may also like to join with believers in Jerusalem in praying, as Jesus suggests, that their escape from Judea "will not be in the winter, or on a Sabbath."[78] If any of the Ultra-Orthodox decide to flee with the believers, they would have a particular problem on the Sabbath, as they will not travel that day beyond a walk, unless they are convinced it is to save a life.

There is an American ministry with premises in Jerusalem which is planning, at the start of the seven-year agreement, to mail every home in Israel. They intend to send out a timetable of what is ahead with instructions concerning the flight from Jerusalem.[79] We can be praying for good relationships between Messianic leaders and such ministries.

When we pray for the *Haredim*, there are different groups to bring before the Lord. They generally are, of course, enthusiastic and devout followers of Judaism. However, there are those within their ranks who are disillusioned with the faith in

---

[77] Genesis 1:28
[78] Matthew 24:20
[79] End Times Inc. founded by the late Irvin Baxter

which they were raised, who are searching for meaning to their lives. They are in a very difficult position because of poverty and the fact that poor secular education inhibits their ability to function well in the job market outside their community. Please pray too for the spread of the Gospel amongst those who make the tough decision to leave the Ultra-Orthodox community in which they grew up, and become secular. This is a lonely path for such people to follow. Then, there are the secret believers in Yeshua who choose to stay within the ranks of the *Haredim*, and we can be praying for them also. Pray for the Messianic communities in Israel to make contact and minister to these various groups.

The ultra-Orthodox are not the only ones aware of the paradox of adhering to the Old Testament without temple sacrifices being in place. This same dilemma is also currently faced by those who consider themselves "Torah Observant" or who follow the "Hebrew Roots Movement"[80] to its logical conclusion. It is simply impossible for these well-meaning believers to observe all of the festivals, including the Sabbath, without making the required temple offerings. Please pray for these Messianic and Gentile Christian groups, both within and outside the State of Israel, to gain understanding before the waters are further muddied by the rebuilt temple.

Sabbath	*shabbat*	שַׁבָּת

---

[80] For further information see internet articles: Got Questions "What is the Hebrew Roots Movement?" One for All "Are we under the Sinai law? What is our stance regarding the Torah? " Jews for Jesus "Messianic Jews in Modern Israel."

4: The 70-week Prophecy of Daniel

"Seventy weeks have been decreed for your people and your holy city, to finish the transgression, to make an end of sin, to make atonement for iniquity, to bring in everlasting righteousness, to seal up vision and prophecy and to anoint the most holy place. So you are to know and discern that from the issuing of a decree to restore and rebuild Jerusalem until Messiah the Prince there will be seven weeks and sixty-two weeks; it will be built again…Then after the sixty-two weeks the Messiah will be cut off and have nothing, and the people of the prince who is to come will destroy the city and the sanctuary…And he will make a firm covenant with the many for one week, but in the middle of the week he will put a stop to sacrifice and grain offering…" (Daniel 9:24-27)

Daniel spent much of his adult life serving in the courts of the king of Babylon. One day, while he was studying the writings of the prophet Jeremiah, Daniel came to realise that the 70-year captivity in Babylon was nearing its end.[81] Jeremiah had pleaded with the people to repent and turn from provoking the LORD to anger by going after other gods. He had warned them that failure to mend their ways would lead to them serving the Babylonians for 70 years, during which time the land would lie desolate. Daniel read how Jeremiah reprimanded Judah for their hard-hearted failure to respond to him, to the other prophets and even to the Lord Himself. Over and over again, Jeremiah rebuked the people of Israel[82] with the words "you have not listened."[83]

---

[81] Daniel 9:2; Jeremiah 25:1-11; 2 Chronicles 36:21
[82] godly people from the tribes of Israel joined with Judah, 2 Chronicles 11:13-17;15:9;30:11
[83] Jeremiah 25:3,4,7; 26:5; 29:19; 35:15

42

Daniel's tender-hearted response to his growing understanding of the reasons for the captivity was to devote time to prayer, fasting and repentance on behalf of Israel. He wrote, "So I gave my attention to the Lord God to seek Him by prayer and supplications, with fasting, sackcloth and ashes."[84] As a godly and sensitive man, he felt distressed and ashamed of the attitudes and behaviour of rebellious Israel which had led to the exile. Daniel was deeply moved by his longing for Israel to depart from their sinful ways and to walk on the path of righteousness. God deeply valued the response of Daniel, just as He showed favour to those who had sighed and cried out over the abominations carried out in the temple in Jerusalem.[85]

God subsequently responded to Daniel's intercession by sending the angel Gabriel to visit him with the 70-week prophecy.[86] Gabriel assured Daniel that the time would yet come for the sins of Israel to be dealt with, and that this would be followed by a period of everlasting righteousness. Daniel is informed that this wonderful event will take place at the end of 70 *weeks*.[87] Instead of the 70 years spoken of by Jeremiah, we now have 70 *weeks*, with the added complication that each *week* (or *seven*) in these verses represents not seven days but seven years. The mystery presented to Daniel refers to *weeks* of years, rather than of days. This prophecy sets out a timetable for the future, culminating in the Second Coming of Jesus.

We read that starting "from the issuing of a decree to restore and rebuild Jerusalem until Messiah the Prince, there will

---

[84] Daniel 9:3
[85] Ezekiel 9:4
[86] Daniel 8:15, 9:21
[87] Daniel 9:24

be seven weeks and sixty-two weeks." This is a total of 69 *weeks*. We need to bear in mind that the Jewish year is a lunar year and so has 360 days. There are various adjustments made in some years by adding an extra month to keep the festivals at the right time of year. We need to start with the year when the decree was issued to "rebuild Jerusalem." If you look at the chart of Bible chronology provided at the end of this book, you will see reference to the proclamation of Artaxerxes to rebuild Jerusalem in 445 BC. This took place 92 years after Cyrus issued his edict for the rebuilding of the temple in Jerusalem. There are various suggestions as to the reason for the 69 *weeks* being split into two periods, seven and 62 *weeks*. One theory suggests that the end of the seven *weeks* corresponds to the end of the writing of the Old Testament in about 400 BC.[88] Another view is that the seven *weeks* takes us to the time when the rebuilding of the city of Jerusalem and its walls were completed.[89]

The phrase "Messiah the Prince" is believed to refer to the time that Jesus rode into Jerusalem on a donkey as King, and was greeted as such by the crowd who were shouting out, "BLESSED IS THE KING WHO COMES IN THE NAME OF THE LORD." The people recognised this as the fulfilment of Zechariah's prophecy, "Rejoice greatly, O daughter of Zion…behold, your king is coming to you…humble, and mounted on a donkey."[90]

When Gabriel spoke of the Messiah being *cut off*, he was referring to His vicarious death. He went on to explain that

---

[88] neverthirsty.org, *Is it significant the 7 weeks and 62 weeks are separated in Daniel 9:25?*

[89] gracethrufaith.com, *Why the 7 weeks plus the 62 weeks?*

[90] Luke 19:38; see also Psalm 118:26, Zechariah 9:9

following the death of the Messiah, Jerusalem and the temple would be destroyed. This further helps us to understand the 70-week prophecy, as we know that Jesus' crucifixion took place in about the year 30 AD when He was "cut off out of the land of the living."[91] The temple was destroyed 40 years later.

So far, we have considered the first 69 *weeks* of the prophecy. When we look at the events of the 70th *week*, we have to conclude that there will be a gap between the time of the death of Jesus on the Cross and the final seven years which will culminate in Israel achieving "everlasting righteousness." Verse 27 describes the final *week* (seven years). It is halfway through this period that the *Time of Jacob's Trouble* starts. The second half of the final *week* is therefore three-and-a-half years, referred to in the book of Revelation as 1,260 days or as "a time and times and half a time."[92]

The focus of the Bible during the gap between the 69th and 70th week is on the Gentile world. Jesus told His disciples that, following the events which were to take place in AD 70, Jerusalem would be trampled underfoot by the Gentiles until the *Times of the Gentiles* are completed.[93] The *Times of the Gentiles* started in 586 BC when the Babylonians destroyed the temple and conquered the people of Judah, most of whom they took away as captives. At the time Jesus was speaking, this situation was soon to be repeated in AD 70 when the Romans trampled Jerusalem underfoot, destroyed the temple, and took the Jewish people from the Land and scattered them abroad. The *Times of the Gentiles* will end with the defeat of the Antichrist,

---

[91] Isaiah 53:8
[92] Revelation 12:6,14
[93] Luke 21:24

who will first desecrate the temple and take control of it. Even though today Jerusalem is in Jewish hands, the Temple Mount is still under control of the Muslim Gentile world. We are therefore still in the *Times of the Gentiles*.

This term *Times of the Gentiles* is not to be confused with the *fullness of the Gentiles* spoken of by the Apostle Paul. He explains "I do not want you, brethren, to be uninformed of this mystery – so that you will not be wise in your own estimation – that a partial hardening has happened to Israel until the fullness of the Gentiles has come in."[94] This verse speaks of the current age in which Gentile believers are daily being added to the Church. There are at least two views as to when this *Church Age* started. A commonly accepted view is that it began at Pentecost, when the Holy Spirit fell upon the Jewish people gathered in one place. Other commentators emphasise that the *Church Age* is defined as the time when God deals primarily with the Gentiles. This second view would be that the *Church Age* started in AD 70, when Israel was expelled from the Land, 40 years after the death and resurrection of Jesus.

In the Bible, the number 40 is associated with a period of testing. We know that Jesus was tested and tempted by Satan for 40 days. Israel was granted 40 years to reconsider her national response to her promised Messiah. The Talmud[95] narrates that, during the 40 years following AD 30, certain miraculous signs previously associated with the temple ceased.[96] One example relates to *Yom Kippur* (Day of Atonement). The Biblical injunction concerning that day is that two goats be taken. The blood of one of them was to be offered as a sin

[94] Romans 11:25
[95] Book of ancient rabbinic Jewish teachings and commentaries
[96] *The Time of the End*, Tim Warner, pp. 315-316

offering to the LORD within the Holy of Holies, and the second goat, the scapegoat, had to be escorted into the wilderness.[97] Tradition tells us that a strip of wool dyed red was tied on the horns of the scapegoat, or to the door of the Temple. The Talmud narrates that at certain times, such as when the High Priest was *Shimon HaTzaddik* (Simon the Righteous), during the period of Alexander the Great, the red strip would commonly turn white during the *Yom Kippur* ceremony. This was a visual image to the Israelites that their sins were forgiven, in keeping with Isaiah's words, "though your sins are as scarlet, they will be as white as snow; though they are red like crimson, they will be like wool."[98] According to the Talmud, this never happened between AD 30 and AD 70.[99] As believers in Jesus, we understand that following His sacrificial death, only His blood could cover the sins of Israel. When the Jewish religious leadership failed their 40-year period of testing, the Israelites were driven out of the Land by the Romans, and it has been suggested that this was the time that the *Church Age* started.

The *Church Age* will end when the final Gentile is saved before the national repentance of Israel. Paul instructs us that salvation has come to the Gentiles to provoke Israel to jealousy. He goes on to say, "Now if their transgression is riches for the world and their failure is riches for the Gentiles, how much more will their fulfillment be!"[100] The Apostle is teaching that when the Jewish people rejected their Messiah, this resulted in the blessings of salvation among the Gentiles, when God turned His attention to them for a season. Paul is telling us that when salvation comes to national Israel, the blessings

---

[97] Leviticus 16
[98] Isaiah 1:18
[99] Talmud, Tractate Yoma 39b
[100] Romans 11:11-12

will be even deeper. We can understand from Paul's comments that the salvation of the Gentiles is not an end in itself, but rather a means to an end. That end will be the national salvation of surviving Israel following the *Time of Jacob's Trouble*.

As we consider this amazing 70-week prophecy, you may find yourself wondering why these prophetic truths are not more apparent to Jewish Biblical scholars. The Hebrew Bible is known as the *Tanakh*. This term is formed from the initials of each of its three divisions. **T**orah is the law of Moses (the first five books of the Bible), **N**eviim are the prophets, and **K**etuvim the writings. The prophets include Isaiah, Jeremiah, Hosea, and Zechariah. The writings include poetic books such as Psalms, Proverbs and Song of Solomon, as well as historical books like Ezra, Nehemiah, and Chronicles. When the Jewish authorities finalised the arrangement of the books in the Hebrew Scriptures, the book of Daniel was placed within the historical writings rather than among the prophets, even though Daniel points the reader precisely to the time of Jesus the Messiah. Reading the 70 weeks of Daniel prophetically would direct Jewish people to the exact timing of the first advent of the Messiah. Jesus accepted Daniel as a prophet, for He referred to *the prophet Daniel* in the New Testament.[101] The Jewish attitude to the last few verses of Isaiah 52 and the whole of Isaiah 53 is similar. These are left out of the Sabbath readings in the synagogue on the grounds that they may cause the people there to think of Jesus.

Jewish scholars have a fascination with numbers in the Bible. The basis of this is that each letter in the Hebrew alphabet has a numerical value. This in turn provides a value for a whole

---

[101] Matthew 24:15

word called the *Gematria*.[102] This is used by Jewish mystics who practise *Kabbalah*[103] as a dubious Biblical interpretation tool. We can be praying that instead of going down a rabbit warren of questionable and distracting interpretations, these students will be drawn to the unambiguous trail laid by Daniel to point to the King Messiah, Yeshua.

Jesus gives us the formula for forgiving our brother "up to seventy times seven."[104] Instead of counting up to 490, we can remember the seventy sevens of Daniel and understand that we need to go on forgiving until the end of this age!

one week	*shavoah echad*	שָׁבוּעַ אֶחָד

---

[102] One example is the word "khai" meaning life. It is spelt with two Hebrew letters, khet and yod. The combined value of the letters is 18, which in turn is regarded as an auspicious number.
[103] A search for the mystic link between the eternal God and the universe
[104] Matthew 18:22

5: The Prophetic Calendar

"I will go away and return to My place, until they acknowledge their guilt and seek My face; in their affliction they will earnestly seek Me…He has torn us, but He will heal us; He has wounded us, but He will bandage us. He will revive us after two days; He will raise us up on the third day, that we may live before Him." (Hosea 5:15 to 6:2)

Hosea instructs us concerning the length of the long gap following the 69th week of Daniel. Instead of *weeks,* we are looking at *days.* The Hebrew word for *day* is *yom,* as we see in *Yom Kippur* (Day of Atonement). Significantly, according to the context of a given verse, English translations of the Hebrew Old Testament translate the word *yom* into one of many different periods of time. In the creation account in Genesis, the word *yom* is translated as *day,* as it evidently refers to a 24-hour day. We know this, because each *yom* is qualified with the words "there was evening and there was morning." In 1 Kings 1:1, the Hebrew reads that King David was advanced in *yamim (days).* This is translated as *years* due to the context.

There is much in the prophetic Scriptures about the period of God's judgement upon the world during the last days. The term used by the prophets is *day of the Lord* (Yom Jehovah).[105] The context makes it clear that this *yom* is not a 24-hour day. Isaiah describes a glorious and beautiful period of the rule of the Branch, the Messiah, following a harrowing period of tribulation, akin to the Holocaust.[106] This will be a time of great fruitfulness. He refers to this occurring *on that day* (b'yom ha-hu). It is not a literal 24-hour period, but the 1,000-year

---

[105] Amos 5:18-20; Zephaniah 1
[106] Isaiah 3:24 to 4:2

millennial reign of Jesus, and again we can see this from the context.

Hosea 6:2 speaks of the third *yom* on which God will raise Israel up, so that they may live before Him. Israel as a nation has never so far walked with the Lord in humble repentance beyond a faithful remnant.[107] What period of time could God be referring to for this national revival after two days, to be followed by a period of obedience? What does *yom* mean here? Such a time is plainly still future. This time of Israel's obedience will last for the 1,000 years known as the *Millennium*. This, in turn, suggests that the preceding two *days,* during which time Israel will wait for this event, is 2,000 years. This is the approximate length of the interval between when Jesus ascended into heaven and the time when He will return to set up His millennial kingdom. This interpretation of Hosea is only acceptable among those who believe that the 1,000 years in Revelation 20 is a literal, rather than a symbolic, period.[108]

These thoughts dovetail with what Hosea says in the first part of the passage about going away. He can be understood to be saying that the Lord will ascend into the heavens for 2,000 years. The *guilt* is the rejection by the Jewish religious leadership of the Messiahship of Jesus. The affliction of the *Time of Jacob's Trouble* is still to come, followed by the raising up of the nation of Israel for the Millennium. We are very close to 2,000 years since the *cutting off,* or death of the Messiah.

This understanding fits with the traditional Jewish view of the millennial week set out in the Talmud and other places. This is based on an ancient understanding of the significance

---

[107] Romans 11:5
[108] mysteryofisrael.org, Reggie Kelly, *How Close are we?*; Hosea 5:14 to 6:2

of the days of the week, as contained within the Ten Commandments. The instruction there is to labour for only six days and to rest on the seventh, as God rested after the six days of creation. Each day is understood to correspond to 1,000 years. We should remember the Apostle Peter teaching that, with the Lord, one day is like a thousand years.[109]

Talmudic Jewish rabbis expect the Messianic Age to last 1,000 years, and to commence 6,000 years after creation. Moses Maimonides, a medieval Jewish rabbi and philosopher of the 12th century, calculated that creation took place in the year 3761 BC. James Ussher, the 17th century Church of Ireland Archbishop of Armagh, reckoned the year of creation to be 4004 BC. We cannot use either figure as basis for a precise calculation relating to the End Times, because of various problems in estimating the date of creation by solely retracing the genealogies in the Torah.

Interestingly, allowing for 6,000 years from the dates for creation suggested by Maimonides and Ussher would place the start of the Millennium between 1996 and 2239. We can see that the last days are drawing near. Might it be that 6,000 years since the actual date of creation coincides exactly with 2,000 years since Jesus was *cut off*?

In this discussion, we are not seeking to be unwise date-setters. Instead, we are endeavouring to emphasise the urgency and closeness of the End Times. We may well feel uncomfortable considering when future events will happen because of the words of the Lord Jesus, "But of that day and hour no one knows, not even the angels of heaven, nor the Son, but the

---

[109] 2 Peter 3:8

Father alone."[110] We will examine the Feast of Trumpets, also known as *Yom Teruah* (*Rosh HaShanah*). Why is it believed by some that the "last trump"[111] and the Rapture of the saints will take place on this day? Why would Jesus use a phrase about no one knowing the *day and hour,* and does it bring to mind the Feast of Trumpets?[112]

Yom Teruah marks the start of the Jewish civil new year. *Teruah* means blowing, as it is the day of the blowing of the ram's horn trumpet, the *Shofar.* The feast starts on the first day of the Jewish month of *Tishri.* The Jewish calendar is lunar, and so that day depends on the sighting of a part of the new moon. In New Testament times, two witnesses had to report to the *Sanhedrin*[113] in Jerusalem that they had seen a fragment of the new moon. If the sky was cloudy, then *Yom Teruah* would need to be postponed until the following day. Therefore, no one could be sure on which day it would occur.

In Psalm 81 we read, "Blow the trumpet at the new moon... on our feast day."[114] The Talmud comments on this verse, "Sound the shofar to mark the new month, the time of concealment."[115] Indeed, the Orthodox today refer to *Rosh HaShanah* as the "day of concealment."[116] Furthermore, the conservative Christian biblical commentators Keil and Delitzsch[117] point out that the new moon is a time when the

---

[110] Matthew 24:36
[111] 1 Corinthians 15:52
[112] Leviticus 23:23-25
[113] The Jewish ruling council in the time of Jesus
[114] Psalm 81:3 (Psalm of Asaph)
[115] Beitzah 16b
[116] Chabad.org "A Day of Concealment" Eliyahu Kitov. Internet article
[117] Franz Delitzsch also translated the Greek New Testament into Hebrew

moon hides itself.[118] So we are starting to see a hint of the uncertainty surrounding the occurrence of this day.

Another clue linking the Feast of Trumpets to the Rapture is that there have traditionally been three named trumpets in the Jewish calendar. One of these is blown at the Feast of Trumpets and is called the "last trump," itself a synonym for *Yom Teruah*.[119] This fits with the Apostle Paul speaking of the Rapture taking place when the last trump sounds.

There is New Testament precedence for this line of reasoning, since the First Coming of Jesus was fulfilled on the dates in the Jewish calendar of the spring festivals. Not only is Jesus our Passover Lamb,[120] but He was crucified at the time of the Passover. Jesus died on the Cross during a period of darkness, just like the innocent Passover lambs were killed at twilight.[121] Paul tells us that Jesus is the *firstfruits* of those who have fallen asleep. Furthermore, He rose from the dead early in the morning on the day of the Feast of Firstfruits.[122] This feast marked the start of the spring barley harvest. 50 days later came the Old Testament feast of *Shavuot* (Pentecost), marking the beginning of the summer wheat harvest.[123] We read in Acts 2:1, "When the day of Pentecost had come..." Here the Greek word for "come" means "to fill completely" with respect to counting down the days. In Jerusalem, the Holy Spirit was poured out on the apostles for the first time at Pentecost. The

---

[118] Biblical Commentary on the Old Testament, section on Psalm 81
[119] Full explanation including Jewish reference material (Theodore Gaster, *Festivals of the Jewish Year*, Herman Kieval *The High Holy Days*) is in the internet article "Rosh HaShanah" at www.mayimhayim.org, chapter 7 by Eddie Chumney
[120] 1 Corinthians 5:7
[121] Exodus 12:6; Matthew 27:45
[122] 1 Corinthians 15:20; Leviticus 23:9-14
[123] Exodus 34:22. The Feasts of the Lord: Kevin Howard, Marvin Rosenthal

harvest that day was the 3,000 souls who responded to Peter's powerful sermon.[124]

The prophetic calendar is set out in Leviticus 23. There is a long, hot, arid gap in the year between the spring festivals[125] representing the First Coming of Jesus, and the three autumn feasts that point to the Second Coming. The first of these autumn festivals is the Feast of Trumpets, which many believe will be prophetically fulfilled by the Church being raptured on that very day of the Hebrew calendar. Each Jewish year, this is followed ten days later by the Day of Atonement, *Yom Kippur*, which typifies the yet-future national repentance of Israel. Finally, we come to the Feast of Tabernacles, *Sukkot*, representing the Messiah's future millennial reign. The long summer interval in the Jewish calendar between the spring and autumn festivals corresponds to the period of time between the resurrection of Jesus (at the end of the 69th week of Daniel) and the Rapture of believers (during the 70th week of Daniel).

How can the 70 weeks of Daniel and the Jewish festivals help us to study the End Times?[126] There are two new years in the Hebrew calendar; the biblical new year starts at Passover,[127] whilst the secular new year begins at *Rosh Hashanah*. All Jewish weeks of years (seven-year periods) start on *Rosh HaShanah*, which occurs each year in late September. The final week of Daniel will be no different. The desecration of the Tribulation Temple by the Antichrist will then occur three-and-a-half years

---

[124] Acts 2:1-13
[125] There is also the Feast of Unleavened Bread during which time Jesus was in the grave. It represents His sinless life. Leviticus 23:6
[126] Explained in detail in the Nelson Walters YouTube video, "The Tribulation is About to Start on this EXACT DAY according to the Bible"
[127] Exodus 12:2

later. The Rapture of the Church is also expected to occur at *Rosh HaShanah* during the final week of Daniel. We can extrapolate from this that the Tribulation subsequently ends at least one year, 10 days later at *Yom Kippur* (corresponding to the national conversion of Israel). The reason it cannot take place on *Yom Kippur* in the same year is because this would only allow for a period of 10 days between the two events. However, when God's wrath is poured out on the post-rapture world in the trumpet and bowl judgements, the fifth trumpet alone lasts for a full five months.[128]

On which annual Feast of Trumpets during the final seven years of this age will the Rapture occur? The answer depends on what the Bible means by the coming wrath of God: "wait for His Son from heaven... *that is,* Jesus who rescues us from the wrath to come."[129] "God has not destined us for wrath, but for obtaining salvation through our Lord Jesus Christ."[130] Christians who believe the Rapture will occur immediately before the final week of Daniel hold to a "pre-tribulation" Rapture. This view places the Rapture before the seal, trumpet and bowl judgements – all of which are understood here to be the wrath of God. Others, including myself, contend that only the trumpet and bowl judgements (but not the prior seal judgements) comprise the wrath of God. This in turn places the Rapture at the time of the sixth seal,[131] just before the seventh seal is broken and the ensuing trumpet judgements. Indeed, immediately following the sixth seal, we read of people hiding and saying to the mountains and rocks, "Fall on us and hide us from the presence of Him who sits on the throne, and from

---

128 Revelation 9:5
129 1 Thessalonians 1:10
130 1 Thessalonians 5:9
131 Revelation 6:12-15

the wrath of the Lamb; for the great day of their wrath has come, and who is able to stand?"[132] Could the terror of the sixth seal be compounded by bearing witness to the resurrection of the physical bodies of those who have died in Christ, as well as the sudden snatching up of the saints?[133]

Yet another view you may come across is that the Rapture will occur after the final trumpet judgement. We are told to expect it, "at the last trumpet; for the trumpet will sound, and the dead will be raised imperishable, and we will be changed."[134] Then again, "the Lord Himself will descend from heaven with a shout, with the voice of the archangel and with the trumpet of God, and the dead in Christ will rise first."[135] Now, there are other trumpets in the Bible apart from those sounded to herald the trumpet judgements in the book of Revelation. For example, the LORD told Moses, "Make yourself two trumpets of silver, you shall make them of hammered work; and you shall use them for summoning the congregation and breaking camp."[136] The Rapture will indeed be the time for believers to instantaneously break camp at the final trump, but this is *not* the same as the last trumpet judgement. Interestingly, between the sixth and seventh trumpet judgements, seven peals of thunder will sound, and yet John was forbidden to write down what he heard.[137] We simply do not know what woes each of these thunders will proclaim on the earth, and the reason why God chose not to reveal any details about them.

---

[132] Revelation 6:16,17
[133] 1 Thessalonians 4:16
[134] 1 Corinthians 15:52
[135] 1 Thessalonians 4:16
[136] Numbers 10:2
[137] Revelation 10:3-4

A further clue to the Rapture's timing is the Lord's teaching about two being in the field, two grinding and two being in a bed.[138] "For as in those days before the flood they were eating and drinking, marrying and giving in marriage, until the day that Noah entered the ark and they did not understand until the flood came and took them all away; so will the coming of the Son of Man be."[139] These activities are all innately mundane, and so suggest that Jesus will rescue His followers before the devastation of the trumpet and bowl judgements – some would argue before the earlier seal judgements too. Nevertheless, there is also a view that the Rapture will take place at the end of the final week of Daniel, after all the judgements are finished; this position is the "post-tribulation Rapture."

After Jesus' resurrection, He indicated to His disciples that it was not for them to know the future times or seasons.[140] However, now that the very time of the end is drawing near, there is an urgent need for watchmen to be vigilant in the same way a New Testament householder would have been, if he knew in advance during which watch of the night the thief was coming.[141] The Roman soldiers divided the night into four three-hour watches.[142] Luke speaks of a faithful and an evil servant awaiting their master's return from a wedding. Jesus explains how the master would be pleased if he returned during the second or third watch of the night and found them on duty.[143] This would be between 9pm and 3am. Jesus walked

---

[138] Matthew 24:41, Luke 17:34-37
[139] Matthew 24:38-39
[140] Acts 1:7
[141] Matthew 24:43
[142] *The Time of the End*, Tim Warne
[143] Luke 12:38-39

towards His disciples on the waters of the Sea of Galilee during the fourth watch of the night between 3am and 6am.[144] Intercessors will be familiar with the instruction of Jesus to watch and pray.[145] Today, apocalyptic watchmen need to identify the signs to watch for and warn of the nearness of the day.

Attempts to date-set can be clumsy. Adding 2,000 years to the most likely date of Jesus' crucifixion still would not supply the day and the hour of the Second Coming. We have not even started looking at how reliable our western Gregorian calendar is when used to date Biblical events. The purpose of this chapter is not to attempt to exactly calculate that day and hour. Rather, we are seeking to learn how to discern these prophetic signs, just as we anticipate the weather.[146] As intercessors, we must appreciate the urgency of the call to prayer and embrace it as the prophetic burden of our generation.

Isaiah describes the duties of a watchman as standing continually on his watchtower during the daytime and sitting at his post every night.[147] If the Lord is calling you to watch and pray in these last days, know that this is a profound responsibility. If in Biblical times the watchman was slack, the entire city would be at risk. Watch for Israel's coming time of trouble, whilst being mindful of the meaning of the final *week* of Daniel and the *days* referred to by Hosea.

day	*yom*	יוֹם

---

[144] Matthew 14:22-33
[145] Mark 13:33; Luke 21:36
[146] Luke 12:56
[147] Isaiah 21:8

6: Bible Mysteries

"But as for you, Daniel, conceal these words and seal up the book until the end of time; many will go back and forth, and knowledge will increase…Go your way, Daniel, for these words are concealed and sealed up until the end time." (Daniel 12:4,9)

The book of Daniel is sealed until the time of the end. Isaiah had previously referred to the general mystery of sealed writings when he wrote to his people, "The entire vision will be to you like the words of a sealed book, which when they give it to the one who is literate, saying 'Please read this,' he will say, 'I cannot, for it is sealed.'"[148] Biblical scholars have identified ancient events from Daniel's timeline, enabling us to interpret one *week* (or seven) as representing seven years. The prophecy was to be a mystery until those who study the Bible used their eyes to run *back and forth* over the book of Daniel. As this intensifies, knowledge about the End Times is increasing.[149]

We can see that Daniel had severe and prolonged physical reactions to the visions he received. We read of him fainting and being ill, his thoughts troubling him and his face growing pale, having no strength, trembling, and being weak and overwhelmed with anguish.[150] Much later, John also reacted to a vision in an extreme manner, "When I saw Him, I fell at His feet like a dead man."[151] These godly men felt overawed, dev-

---

[148] Isaiah 29:11
[149] See "Daniel Unsealed" by Nelson Walters and Bob Brown published by Ready for Jesus Publications (Wilmington, NC,2018)
[150] Daniel 8:27; 7:28; 10:8; 10:11,16
[151] Revelation 1:17

astated and horrified by what they saw and heard. As intercessors for Israel, we too will find our hearts deeply moved by the troubling matters concerning the *Time of Jacob's Trouble*.

We are told in the book of Daniel that, during "the end time," there will be those who understand what is going on, and they will teach many. The insight of the wise is contrasted to the lack of understanding of the wicked.[152] When you consider how seldom eschatological matters are taught in many Christian circles, and the importance of this subject, you can appreciate the potential value of these wise teachers currently being prepared by the Lord. We can be praying for God to raise up more of these teachers and to deepen their understanding of the prophetic Scriptures. The time for their ministry is still future, and their role will not be easy, as at least some "will fall by sword and by flame, by captivity and by plunder for many days."

Unsealing the book of Daniel is in keeping with the theme running throughout Scripture of divine revelation of Biblical truths previously hidden. In the Old Testament, such truths are described as *dark sayings* or *riddles*.[153] The New Testament refers to *mysteries* in various passages.[154] In both Testaments we are speaking of something hidden, which is then revealed by God. It is not obvious to the casual reader. The Greek word *musterion* in the New Testament speaks of a secret matter which will only be disclosed to the initiated. It implies a secret being shared rather than a complex enigma being explained. This may remind you of the parables of Jesus, which He spoke to

---

[152] Daniel 11:33-35, 12:10
[153] Numbers 12:8; Psalm 49:4, 78:2; Proverbs 1:6
[154] Ephesians 1:9, 3:9, 5:32; Romans 11:25-27; 2 Thessalonians 2:7; Timothy 3:16

hide the meaning to those not given the privilege of understanding kingdom matters.[155]

It is as though the Scriptures are a lovely lush, carefully planted garden, with gold chunks, precious jewels, gems, and pearls hidden beneath the surface of the soil, to be gradually dug up and examined. The verses analogous to the lovely visible flowers include such passages as the description of true love in 1 Corinthians 13, and the comforting words of Psalm 23. Even those who do not know the Lord are touched by moving passages such as Ecclesiastes 3:1-8, which include the profound words, "There is an appointed time for everything. And there is a time for every event under heaven – a time to give birth and a time to die." However, we all need to take time and effort to dig deep to reveal the gemstones and other relevant teachings. In His rich love for us, the Lord has laid up so much for us in His word.[156]

We may like to think about why God speaks in such a mysterious manner, especially about the End Times, and why it can be a struggle to wrap our heads around the details. Perhaps there have been occasions in your life, as you look back, when God was leading you in a manner which only became apparent over time. If so, you may have some thoughts on why this happens. A helpful verse concerning these gradually unravelling mysteries is Habakkuk 2:3, where it says: "for the vision is yet for the appointed time; it hastens toward the goal and it will not fail. Though it tarries, wait for it; for it will certainly come, it will not delay." The book of Daniel has hidden depths which will become understandable as it is progressively unsealed. Another Scripture for us to bear in mind is, "It is the

---

155 Matthew 13:13
156 Matthew 13:52

glory of God to conceal a matter, but the glory of kings is to search out a matter."[157] We therefore should be diligent in seeking to understand the End Times.

We have already alluded as to how the Lord Jesus answered the disciples when they asked, after His resurrection, if it was the time for Him to restore the kingdom to Israel. Jesus replied, "It is not for you to know times or epochs which the Father has fixed by His own authority."[158] Perhaps His reply makes more sense to our minds with the perspective that some matters are only gradually revealed. It is not the question that was wrong; we read of Isaiah asking the Lord how long it would be before judgement came to the Jewish nation.[159] What was wrong was the expectation that the answer would be supplied before the time was ripe. As the time draws near, the answer will become clearer to the appointed watchmen. The Greek word *kairous*, translated *epoch* in Jesus' reply, means *season*. Solomon instructs us in the book of Ecclesiastes that for everything there is a season. This is the season for the watchmen to understand the signs of the time and that the Day is drawing near.

The books of Daniel and Revelation are known as *apocalyptic literature*. This term comes from the Greek word for revelation, *apocalypse*. Seeing what the writers of these two books have in common is instructive. At the time of their respective writings, Daniel was about 85 and John well into his 90s. Daniel had been taken away captive as a youth from Judea to Babylon, where he served in the royal court. John had been imprisoned by the Romans as an old man on the Isle of Patmos.

[157] Proverbs 25:2
[158] Acts 1:6-7
[159] Isaiah 6:11

The Lord had a very special regard for them both. Daniel is referred to in words suggesting *highly valued* and John as one "whom Jesus loved."[160]

We can take encouragement from their intimate relationship with the Lord, as well as from their ages. We may be struck by the degree of suffering each had to go through. We know that Daniel was thrown into the lions' den. John introduces himself as one who knows suffering, "I, John, your brother and fellow partaker in the tribulation and kingdom and perseverance which are in Jesus."[161] Our relationship with the Lord may well deepen as our intercession for Israel draws us to seek and share more of His heart.

As you consider this chapter, you may be moved to go on praying for the mysteries of the Gospel of Yeshua in the Old Testament to be revealed to the Ultra-Orthodox whose life's mission is to study the Torah and Talmud. To encourage you, consider the case of the Ultra-Orthodox rabbi, *Yitzhak Kaduri* from the *Sephardic*[162] community. He is reputed to have left a note to be opened one year after his death in 2006, revealing the name of the Messiah. The note said the name was *Yehoshua* (Joshua), which is the longer name from which the name *Yeshua* (Jesus) is derived.

Daniel	דָּנִיֵּאל

---

160 Daniel 9:23, 10:11; John 13:23
161 Revelation 1:9
162 Jewish people and their descendants who came to Israel from places like Spain, Portugal, the Middle East and North Africa. By contrast, the Ashkenazi Jews come from other parts of Europe and the USA.

7: A Statue and Beasts

"O LORD our God, other masters besides You have ruled us."
(Isaiah 26:13)

Each Passover, Jewish people gather in their homes to celebrate the wonderful ancient delivery from slavery in Egypt. This pattern of subjugation followed by deliverance was to be repeated throughout the history of the nation, and will indeed continue into the future. Following the exodus from Egypt, Israel was subsequently oppressed, in a less severe manner, by rulers of other areas such as Mesopotamia, Moab, Canaan and Midian.[163] Isaiah wrote warning of the impending invasion by the Assyrians.[164] It is believed that Chapters 36-38 of his book were written at the time of the Assyrian invasion.

Over a century later, the Babylonians[165] invaded the Land. The prophet Jeremiah was scorned when he foretold the fall of Jerusalem at the hands of the Babylonians. Nearly 50 years later, the Medo-Persians[166] under their ruler Cyrus, conquered the city of Babylon, taking over the empire and thus becoming *master* over Israel. The book of Esther is set during the time of the Medo-Persian Empire. The Greeks, under Alexander the Great, invaded Israel during the intertestamental period.[167] By the time of Jesus' youth, the Romans[168] were the *masters*. They

---

[163] Judges 3:8,14, 4:2, 6:1
[164] Isaiah 7:17, 8:4-8. The Assyrian Empire included at its height: Iraq, Israel, Lebanon, Syria, Cyprus and large parts of Iran, Turkey and Egypt.
[165] The Babylonian Empire covered Iraq, Syria, Lebanon, Israel, Cyprus, Jordan, and parts of Egypt, Turkey, Iran and Saudi Arabia
[166] The Medo-Persian Empire covered Iran, Cyprus, Syria, Israel, Lebanon and parts of Jordan, Iraq, Egypt, Armenia, Azerbaijan and Turkmenistan
[167] The gap between the end of the Old Testament and the start of the New Testament, known as *the 400 years of silence*
[168] The Roman Empire covered most of Europe and the Middle East and the north coast of Africa

made full occupation of the Land in AD 6, replacing the Herodian rule. Following the Romans, a number of invaders took over Israel's territory, including Persians, Arabs, Turks, Crusaders and Egyptians. Then, the giant Ottoman Empire[169] absorbed it in 1517, holding it for 400 years. Details of relevant dates and how they correspond to the Bible are provided in the first of the two charts at the back of this book.

Daniel Chapter 2 relates to the troubling dream of King Nebuchadnezzar. The secret of the dream was revealed to Daniel in a night vision. He was able to both describe the dream of a statue with a head of gold and explain to the king what each part of the statue represented. The statue is, in effect, a three-dimensional history timeline that stretches from the Babylonian Empire to the Second Coming of Jesus.

If you start at the head and look *down* the body of the statue, like Daniel did, you are going from the time when King Nebuchadnezzar was ruler of the Babylonian Empire, *down* through the centuries to the return of the Lord Jesus. If you look *up* the body from the feet, you are going back in time from the Second Coming, *up* through the centuries, all the way to the Babylonian Empire, whose king Daniel served.

The statue is an unstable construction, with its heavy head of gold, going *down* to its feet made of a combination of iron and clay. As you go *down* the body, the metals become less valuable, and this in turn suggests a decline in the magnificence of the empires being represented. Daniel tells Nebuchadnezzar, ruler of the Babylonian Empire, that he is the head of gold (verse 38). Daniel explains that the kingdom which will follow

---

[169] The Ottoman Empire covered large areas of West Asia, south-eastern Europe and North Africa

will be inferior to Nebuchadnezzar's (verse 39). This is reflected in the fact that silver is less costly than gold. Biblical scholars generally agree that this kingdom of silver refers to the Medo-Persian Empire. In fact, Daniel lived to see the transition of power from the Babylonians to the Medo-Persians and served in the court of Darius the Mede.[170]

The third kingdom in the statue, which is represented by bronze, is the Greek Empire of Alexander the Great. We are told that this bronze empire will rule over all the earth. This is Middle Eastern hyperbole.[171] Alexander the Great's empire never stretched literally over the whole world. We had the same hyperbole earlier in verse 38 where Daniel told Nebuchadnezzar that wherever people were living, and wherever there were birds and animals, there he was the ruler. We know that the Babylonian Empire also was not literally worldwide.

The two legs of iron refer to the fourth empire, which comes after the bronze Greek Empire. We can see from verse 40 that the legs of iron will dominate and crush all the others. Next, coming out of the legs are "the feet and toes, partly of potter's clay and partly of iron." We are told that there will be a weakness due to a lack of cohesion in this final empire "even as iron does not combine with pottery."[172] We see that these two empires are somehow related because they both contain iron.

There is a divergence of opinion as to which empire the iron legs represent. Consideration of this is far from an academic exercise. The area of the world to which we prayerfully

---

[170] Daniel 11:1
[171] *Mid-East Beast*, Joel Richardson, pp. 49-50
[172] Daniel 2:41-43

look for the rise of the future Antichrist will depend on our understanding of this matter. The traditional view is that it is the Roman Empire, which was ruling over Israel at the time of Jesus' First Coming. Adherents of this view would say that the subsequent iron and clay mixture, coming out of the legs, refers to a revived end-times Roman Empire. This has been understood as a European coalition such as the European Economic Community. The weakness of the feet is seen to point to the intrinsic cultural and linguistic differences between the nations in Europe. Clearly, those with this understanding will keep a prayerful watch upon events and leaders in Europe. Many commentators have worked from the head of the statue *downwards* and looked at what succeeded the Greek Empire. This has led to an entirely logical conclusion that the legs are the Roman Empire.

A luxury we have in these End Times is to consider the statue working *upwards*, starting with the feet, which represent the end-times ruling power. This leads to the alternate view that the iron legs refer to the Ottoman Empire, rather than to the Roman Empire.[173] If we look back in history, we see that the Ottoman Empire was the empire which most recently controlled the land of Israel, between 1517 and 1917. It was a vast empire centred in Turkey. This in turn places the feet of iron and clay as part of a revived Ottoman Empire. A revived Islamic Ottoman *caliphate*[174] may relate to the unstable feet of the statue, as there are two distinct groups of Muslims: the Sunnis and the Shia. They do not mix well with one another, given

---

[173] See Further Resources on page 158 for the teachings of Joel Richardson (Joel's Trumpet) and David Rosenthal (Zion's Hope)
[174] Lands governed by Islamic law, led by a Caliph

that they have had strong differences for centuries. The Ottoman Empire was a Sunni *caliphate*. The adherents to this view will be looking to Asia Minor for the rise of the Antichrist.

There are parallel passages in Daniel and Revelation where the imagery changes, and instead of these empires being represented by parts of a statue, they are portrayed as animals, or *beasts*.[175] I have provided a second chart at the end of this book, entitled *Chart of Beast Empires*. This uses the parts of the statue in Daniel 2 as a framework on which to hang the creatures and their horns referred to in these other passages.

In Daniel 7:1-8, the mighty Babylonian empire is this time depicted as a lion rather than as a head of gold. The Medo-Persian Empire is a bear. The Greek Empire, which rapidly advanced, is presented to us as being like a leopard with wings. The empire which follows these is not identified biologically as a specific creature, but rather as being "dreadful and terrifying and extremely strong; and it had large iron teeth." It was savage to those around. This fourth beast has ten *horns*, which become dominated and defeated by a *little horn*, who we know to be the Antichrist. We learn later from Daniel 7:24 that the ten *horns* are ten kings. This end-times group of leaders corresponds to the ten toes of the statue in Daniel Chapter 2.

The initial fulfillment of the *little horn* in the book of Daniel is thought to be Antiochus Epiphanes IV, born around 215 BC.[176] The empire of Alexander the Great was split into various areas after his untimely early death. The ruler of one of these was Antiochus Epiphanes IV. He is considered a type of

---

[175] Daniel 7:1-8, 8; Revelation 13, 17:7-14
[176] Daniel 7:8, 8:9

the Antichrist, even down to desecrating the temple in Jerusalem. There are many similarities between Antiochus Epiphanes IV and the coming Antichrist. The name Antiochus comes from the Greek word *anti* meaning *like, compared to,* or *in place of.* It is the same Greek word used in the title *Antichrist.* The title "Epiphanes" means *god manifest.* He was *in place of god manifest* and the Antichrist will be *in place of Christ.* Antiochus was responsible for a severe persecution of the Jewish people in Israel, making adherence to the Jewish faith and religious customs illegal, forbidding the Israelites to circumcise their sons or to observe the Sabbath. He desecrated the temple in Jerusalem by offering a pig to Zeus on the altar of incense. Pigs are, of course, unclean animals to Jewish people.[177]

Judas Maccabee led a three-year Jewish revolt against Antiochus Epiphanes, after which time his forces were able to take back the city of Jerusalem and rededicate the temple. This continues to be remembered each year by Jewish people at *Hanukkah.* We read about this feast of *Hanukkah* in John 10:22, where we are told about Jesus being in the temple courts during the winter, at the time of the Feast of Dedication. Antiochus Epiphanes failed to destroy Israel and the Jewish people in his cruel zeal to promote himself and the Greek culture. In the same way, the coming Antichrist will not succeed in wiping out Israel.

The vision of the ram and goat of Daniel 8 involves only two of the beast empires that have ruled over Israel. This time the Medo-Persian Empire is portrayed as a ram (rather than a bear) and the ancient Greek empire as a goat (not a leopard). We see Alexander the Great as the large *horn* (or king) in verse

---

[177] Leviticus 11:7-8

8, and commentators liken the four notable *horns* (or kings) that grew in his place to the four rulers who arose after his death. Then once again, we have the picture of a *little horn*, this time growing out of one of the four horns. This *little horn* is the Antichrist typified by Antiochus Epiphanes IV.

There is a very helpful teaching video by Nelson Walters, founder and director of "Last Days Overcomers," shedding light on this vision.[178] The victory of Greece (the goat) over Persia (the ram) was merely an early partial fulfillment of this prophecy. The video points out that Daniel is told three times how the vision of the ram and goat in Daniel 8 pertains to the time of the end.[179] So we know from this that in the latter days, Iran (the ram) will again push towards the west, north and south.[180] Indeed, Iran, intent on the destruction of Israel, is sponsoring the activities of terrorist groups such as Palestinian Islamic Jihad, Popular Front for the Liberation of Palestine, Hezbollah, and Hamas. These operate in Israel, Lebanon and Syria to the west. Southward, Iran also supports the Houthi rebels in Yemen. However, at the time of writing, we have not yet seen Iran expand northward. We are told in Daniel 8 that the goat (*Yavan*), will be enraged at the ram (Iran) and attack her furiously.[181] A possible reason for the anger may be because Iran will yet promote its own Shiite Mahdi (the Twelfth Imam),[182] or messiah, an action that would be deeply offensive to Turkey and other Sunni Muslim lands.

Could the United Nations decide that the would-be victorious nation of Turkey is too regionally dominant, and pass a

---

[178] Nelson Walters "Where Will the Antichrist Come From According to Daniel" YouTube
[179] Daniel 8:17,19
[180] Daniel 8:4
[181] Daniel 8:6-7
[182] For further details see Chapter 14, page 129

condemnatory resolution, fracturing it into four parts? Out of one of these four, could the Antichrist, or *little horn*, arise?[183] For anyone puzzling how an initial reference to Alexander the Great and his historical Greek empire could equate to Turkey, most Bibles mistranslate the Hebrew word *Yavan* as Greece, whereas in fact the term *Yavan* is believed to indicate western Turkey and eastern Greece. Watching and praying does not only involve seeing how events in the book of Revelation play out. We also must take into account the various clues provided by the prophet Daniel, as well as the other Hebrew prophets.

Revelation 13 portrays a composite beast which arises from the sea. This beast is primarily like a leopard, and so again relates to the Greek Empire. In addition, the beast has feet like those of a bear, and so has associations with the Medo- Persian Empire. It has the mouth of a lion, which connects it to the Babylonian Empire. This ferocious beast is linked to the Middle East nations around Israel, rather than to a European monster. If Turkey (at one stage part of the Greek Empire) succeeds in re-establishing the Ottoman empire as an Islamic *caliphate*, then it could soon look like a menacing beast, especially to the lands around it.

Revelation 17:7-14 sheds light on what John saw in Chapter 13. It speaks of "seven kings; five have fallen, one is, the other has not yet come." Then we are told of an eighth who "is one of the seven." The book of Revelation was written at the time that the Roman Empire ruled over the land of Israel. So, we know that the Roman Empire must be the sixth king, as at the time of the Apostle John writing, it would have been said that the Roman Empire *is*. Then the seventh one is yet to

---

[183] Daniel 8:8-14

come and would be the then-future Ottoman Empire, whose influence you can see in the buildings and architecture in Israel today.

The final *beast*, the one which attacks Israel, to bring about the Great Tribulation, is related to the seven, suggesting continuity with the previous empires. If you go back to Revelation 13:3, you can also see that one of the seven heads is mortally wounded and yet revives into a *beast* out of which comes the Antichrist. Of the seven *beast empires* which have been fatally wounded, which one will yet come back to life to oppress Israel? After approximately a century since being dismantled in the aftermath of World War I, could the answer be that an Islamic *caliphate* will reform out of the ashes of the Ottoman empire?

Prophecy watchers may have been alerted by the election success of Turkey's leader, Recep Tayyip Erdoğan, on 28th May 2023. His long rule started 20 years earlier when he became Prime Minister.[184] This latest result secured him a third term as President. Many contend that he has been changing the fundamentally secular character of Turkey, by imposing a hardline Islamic stance.[185] The Minister of the Interior, Süleyman Soylu, responded to Erdoğan's recent victory with a rousing speech. He is reported to have said that the people did not merely elect a national leader in Erdoğan, but a leader for the

---

[184] huffpost.com "Turkey's Erdogan Wins Another Term As President, Extending Rule Into 3rd Decade." apnews.com: Key dates in the career of Turkey's Recep Tayyip Erdogan
[185] ECPS Erdogan's Political Journey: From Victimised Muslim Democrat to Authoritarian, Islamic Populist. Ihsan Yilmaz. Internet article

world, and that over the following five years, neighbouring [Islamic] countries will join Turkey.[186] Are we perhaps finally witnessing the early stages of the re-emergence of the Ottoman Empire? We will look at the prophesied future invasion of Israel in Chapter 9 of this book. Will Turkey soon forge an alliance with nearby nations to comprise the invading confederacy set out in Ezekiel 38:1-6?

Now that we have briefly considered the two schools of thought as to the identity of the empire represented by the iron legs, certain questions come to mind. Would a European leader have the necessary motivation to force adherents of all faiths, including Muslim people, to follow his one-world religion? Would a *caliph* ruthlessly pursue the spread of radical Islam? Which of these two theories fits better with the agenda of the Antichrist to seek to dominate the world? The prospect of a fundamentalist Islamic army marching into Israel, intent on her destruction, is a chilling image for us to consider, and one to stir the heart of the intercessor.

the earth	*haaretz*	הָאָרֶץ

---

[186] Journalist Abdullah Bozkurt's Twitter account, 28th May 2023, https://twitter.com/abdbozkurt/status/1662916702340886528

8: Deceptions

"false Christs and false prophets will arise and will show great signs and wonders, so as to mislead, if possible, even the elect." (Matthew 24:24)

These words of Jesus about false prophets suggest that Christians who emphasise *signs and wonders* will be particularly vulnerable to the end-times deceptions. This teaching of the Lord is presented to us in the context of the persecution and killing of His followers in the last days. Courage and discernment will be essential for those faced with a choice between severe tribulation and leaving the narrow path to enjoy deceptive *signs and wonders*. This leads us to the warning issued by Paul that the Second Coming will not occur until there is a great apostasy, or *falling away* from the faith, and the Antichrist is revealed.[187] It will not only be church goers who will be beguiled by deceptive *signs and wonders*. Many Israelis already have a fascination with New Age practices and the land of India. As Isaiah said, "they are filled with influences from the east."[188] They will be among those who need prayer for discernment.

There will be other pressures on believers threatening to pull them away from the narrow path during the final *week* of this age. Many will be *offended* by the events ahead.[189] Believers drawn to the prosperity gospel are taught to expect health and wealth. Christians seeking constant blessings and riches will be shocked by the hardships and sufferings during the End Times. This *offence* will lead to disillusionment with the Christian faith. Paul attributes the cause of the deception of lying

---

[187] 2 Thessalonians 2:3-12
[188] Isaiah 2:6
[189] Matthew 24:10 speaks of many professing Christians *falling away* or being *offended*, depending on the Bible translation

signs and wonders to be people not loving the truth.[190] We have to ask ourselves why it is that many people are more easily persuaded by miracles than by the truth of the Word of God. Paul was aware of this, as he observed that "Jews ask for signs."[191] We know that the *falling away* in the End Times will be substantial, since Jesus warns us, "However, when the Son of Man comes, will He find faith on the earth?"[192]

Betrayals will be yet another pressure during the last days. Timothy says that "in the last days difficult times will come," and describes men as being "lovers of self, lovers of money, boastful, arrogant, revilers, disobedient to parents, ungrateful, unholy, unloving, irreconcilable, malicious gossips, without self-control, brutal, haters of good, treacherous, reckless, conceited, lovers of pleasure rather than lovers of God."[193] Jesus warns His disciples that they will be *betrayed* by parents, brothers, relatives and friends.[194] The *offence*, betrayal and hatred in the End Times will be a far cry from unity in the Body, which Jesus prayed for in John 17.

Mocking the belief in the return of Christ is a further characteristic of the End Times for which the godly need to be prepared. Peter instructs us that mockers will be saying, "where is the promise of His coming? For ever since the fathers fell asleep, all continues just as it was from the beginning of creation."[195] The scoffing stems from a poor view of creation and the philosophy of *uniformitarianism*, which views weather conditions and ageing of rocks to have continued at

[190] 2 Thessalonians 2:8-12
[191] 1 Corinthians 1:22
[192] Luke 18:8
[193] 2 Timothy 3:1-4
[194] Luke 21:16
[195] 2 Peter 3:3-9

the same rate over long periods of time. All rock-dating methods assume *uniformitarianism* to be correct. The catastrophic Noahic Flood is not factored in to such an approach. We know that water can cause sudden far-reaching changes in rock appearance and the physical landscape. *Uniformitarians* assume that drastic geological changes, which were actually caused by the Flood, have instead happened gradually over millions of years.

If people do not believe that God created the world, and that He has already acted in severe judgement, then they also will not envisage a sudden end. They certainly would not be expecting Jesus to come again and for this age to be wound up in judgement. They believe that the past, as they perceive it, is the key to the future, and so they mock. Yet Peter warns about a drastic end to the world: fire. A sound view of creation is fundamental to a solid understanding of the future, yet, sadly, the deception of evolution is already firmly in place as we approach the End Times.

We come on to the peace agreement, mentioned in Chapter 3, which the Antichrist will broker between Israel and her enemies. We read that "he will make a firm covenant with the many for one week."[196] All the wars Israel has fought, and all the terrorism and hostility she has endured, are fundamentally because her enemies have refused to accept that Israel has the right to the Land. This situation leaves the Palestinian people in a vulnerable and uncertain position, open to being exploited or radicalised by the enemies of Israel.

This future peace agreement will cause Israelis to breathe a collective sigh of relief. At the time of writing, Israel spends

---

[196] Daniel 9:27

over 4% of its gross domestic product on defence.[197] By contrast, the United Kingdom's figure is under 2%. Finance is not the only societal consideration. Conscription into the Israeli Defence Force (IDF) is compulsory for 18-year-olds, with limited exemptions, such as for married women. Military service places a massive strain upon the families of school-leavers as soldiers are a frequent target of terrorists.

Israelis will embrace the future peace agreement. It will fulfil their yearning for *peace and security*. The prospect of *peace* and scaling back the IDF will be a realisation of a long-held dream. However, if something seems too good to be true, it usually is. The agreement is described in the book of Isaiah as a *covenant with death*.[198] The implication of this phrase is that the whole project will be an impending disaster. Revelation Chapter 6 tells us of *the Four Horsemen of the Apocalypse*. The Antichrist, who will arrange this deal, is represented by the rider of the first horse, the *white horse*.[199] He has a bow but no arrows. This implies that he will conquer through diplomacy, rather than through using the weapons of warfare. He will be a satanic counterfeit of the *Prince of Peace*, the Lord Jesus, who is presented later in the book of Revelation returning on a *white horse*.[200]

The Israelis will initially regard the Antichrist as some sort of saviour. The citizens of Israel have had to endure a series of wars and military conflicts since 1948. Israel contends with terrorists within and outside its borders. However, compared to when the Jewish people lived in Tsarist Russia or in Nazi-

---

[197] Total of value of goods and services provided by a country
[198] Isaiah 28:15,18
[199] Revelation 6:2
[200] Revelation 19:11

occupied Europe, today they live in comparative security in Israel. This is just as Ezekiel describes "the land that is restored from the sword, whose inhabitants have been gathered from many nations…they are living securely, all of them." When this apparent saviour reveals his true intent, three and a half years after the agreement commences, he will be saying to himself, "I will go up against the land of unwalled villages; I will go against those who are at rest, that live securely."[201] The Israelis will have been lulled into a false sense of security. The warning issued by Jeremiah just before the Babylonian invasion will again hold true: "they have healed the brokenness of My people superficially, saying 'Peace, peace,' but there is no peace."[202] The Apostle Paul warns "while they are saying, 'peace and safety!' then destruction will come upon them suddenly like labour pains upon a woman with child, and they will not escape."[203]

We can expect the peace agreement to finally permit Orthodox Jews to reinstate Jewish sacrifices on the Temple Mount. The site already houses two Islamic structures: the Dome of the Rock shrine and the Al-Aqsa Mosque. Tensions run high with protests, riots, and shootings. This dates back to June 1967 when Israel defeated the Jordanians in the Six Day War. At the end of this war the Israeli Defence Minister, Moshe Dayan, conceded control of the Temple Mount to the Jordanians. The Jordanian authorities manage the religious aspect of the area, with Israeli police in charge of access to the site.[204] The Dome of the Rock is widely believed to be on the site of Solomon's Temple, encompassing the very rock on

---

[201] Ezekiel 38:8,11
[202] Jeremiah 6:14
[203] 1 Thessalonians 5:3
[204] AJC Global Voice "What to know about Jerusalem's Temple Mount" internet article.

Mount Moriah where Abraham had previously placed Isaac bound for sacrifice.[205]

The future temple raises all sorts of questions. The issue of temple sacrifices may divide the Messianic Community in Israel. Mainstream believers could challenge *Torah observant Messianic Jews*[206] as to why they are supporting such a venture. What will animal rights activists make of the slaughter of innocent sacrificial creatures? When Jesus cleansed the temple, He drove out those who bought and sold there. He overturned the money changers' tables.[207] We can expect the local tourist market to do a brisk trade in selling wooden carved models of the temple and associated souvenirs. Will there be more offensive commercialisation associated with the site?

There can be no future temple without a *red heifer*. The LORD instructed the children of Israel to make use of a *red heifer* free from any *defect*, whose ashes were to be kept to add to *living water*.[208] These sanctifying waters are necessary to purify the Temple Mount area and the temple vessels. Each member of the Levitical priesthood will also have to be regularly cleansed in such a manner. This is because any individual who has *ever* been rabbinically contaminated by contact with a corpse is forbidden to participate in temple worship. Setting foot in a graveyard, for example, would cause such defilement. Even if a Levite has never been to a graveside, they still must be repeatedly cleansed lest they have inadvertently walked on land where once a dead body lay or on an area beneath which a dead body is buried. The Biblical requirement for a *red heifer*

---

[205] Genesis 22:2, 2 Chronicles 3:1
[206] These Jewish believers in Jesus seek to combine their New Testament faith with Old Testament practices, see page 40
[207] Matthew 21:12-13
[208] Water which flows from a natural spring. Numbers 19:1-22; Hebrews 9:13-14

has previously caused some to dismiss eschatology as a futile search to procure the ashes of a red heifer.

Over recent years, there have been a series of red heifers as potential candidates for this fundamental role in the future Temple. However, under the sovereign will of God, so far each one has disappointed by going on to develop disqualifying white or black hairs. Significantly, on September 15th 2022, five red heifers were flown into Israel from Texas, USA. This is currently causing great excitement in prophetic circles, because of the probability that one will qualify for their ashes to be used in the Temple. As of March 2023, three of the five heifers remain eligible to fulfil the Biblical requirements.[209] Inevitably, as suggested in Chapter 3, there will be deep differences of opinion among evangelical Christians concerning the animal sacrifices to be made in this temple.[210]

In 2019, an ordinary sickly heifer was burned in Israel as an experiment to ascertain how many times people could be sanctified by one *red heifer*. The conclusion was that there would be sufficient drops of the purifying water for at least 660 billion uses!

In the time of the Tabernacle of Moses, the *red heifer* had to be slaughtered outside the camp of Israel.[211] Subsequently, in the temple period, the same pattern was followed. The eventual tenth *red heifer* will also need to be killed outside the city of Jerusalem, as the Lord Jesus died on a cruel Roman cross just beyond the city walls.

---

[209] Nelson Walters You Tube video "Red Heifer-Third Temple Breaking Inside Information Update."
[210] For example, see Nelson Walters You Tube video "Why Doesn't the Antichrist die When He Enters the Third Temple's Holy of Holies?"
[211] Numbers 19:3

The founders of the Temple Institute show us the resolute determination of the Ultra-Orthodox community. The *Haredim* have played a significant role in Israeli government coalitions since the State was established. Yet, at the time of writing, it is still not possible for the temple to be rebuilt. We may marvel at the outworking of the sovereignty of God when we consider the decision of Moshe Dayan, a secular Israeli general. Then, there are the constraints of finding a *red heifer*. Even when the sanctifying elements of the *red heifer* are ready, there will still be one final part of the jigsaw to slot into place. This will be the agreement of the Islamic community to share the Temple Mount site. This will yet be accomplished by the Antichrist.

Pray for the Holy Spirit to work in the hearts of those training and serving in the Temple Institute. May they ponder on the significance of the beautiful, unblemished red heifer. May they understand that the living waters of God sanctify us and deliver us from eternal spiritual death to everlasting life. May they also be so moved by the sacrifice of innocent lambs as to see the death of the Lamb of God on the Cross. May they turn to the One, like a lamb without blemish or spot, who paid the price for our sins, once for all.[212] Pray too for discernment among Messianic Jewish believers, and especially their leaders, in the land of Israel, so they will be wise in their attitude and witness concerning this tribulation temple.

red heifer	*parah adoomah*	פָּרָה אֲדֻמָּה

---

[212] 1 Peter 1:19; Hebrews 10:10

9: The Invasion of Israel

"Son of man, set your face toward Gog of the land of Magog, the prince of Rosh, Meshech and Tubal, and prophesy against him and say, 'Thus says the Lord GOD, "Behold I am against you, O Gog, prince of Rosh, Meshech and Tubal. I will turn you about and put hooks into your jaws..."'' (Ezekiel 38:2-4)

Many readers will have spent time in Israel and marvelled at the sophistication of society, industry, transport, culture, agriculture and infrastructure. All this in a land which only gained its independence as recently as 1948. The ugly prospect of marauding destructive forces invading the "Beautiful Land"[213] is almost unthinkable. Yet we cannot ignore, and must reluctantly digest, the prophetic picture painted in Ezekiel 38-39 and Zechariah 12-14.

The invaders listed by Ezekiel come from places that sound strange to our ears. Broadly speaking, the nations which will lead this invasion are situated to the north of Israel and are descended from Noah's son Japheth.[214] The powerful military leader of the invasion is "Gog of the land of Magog." There is a divergence of opinion as to the location of *Magog*, even in the Jewish world. Moses Maimonides took the view that the term referred to an area on the border between Turkey and Syria.[215] Josephus placed *Magog* within Russia. We read in Ezekiel that the leader *Gog* is "the prince of Rosh, Meshech and Tubal." Some expect *Gog* to originate from a place called *Rosh*, which they identify as *Russia* because of the similarity of sound. Others take the view that *rosh* suggests that *Gog* will be

[213] Daniel 11: 16,41
[214] Genesis 10:2
[215] danieltrainingnetwork.org/gog-antichrist-historical-survey

a *head* prince or leader because the Hebrew word for *head* is *rosh*. We see this in the Hebrew phrase for the Jewish New Year, *Rosh HaShanah,* which literally means *head of the year.* The areas of *Meshech, Tubal, Gomer* and *Togarmah* are generally considered to be within modern-day Turkey. *Persia* is plainly modern-day Iran. *Cush and Ethiopia* point to northern Sudan. *Put* is Libya and may also include other parts of North Africa. We are told that *many peoples* are with Gog.[216] It is possible that jihadists from all parts of the world will join with Turkey, Iran, and other nations in the future invasion of Israel, just as many travelled to fight with the Islamic State in Syria in recent years.

We read that the LORD will put *hooks* in the jaws of the invaders to draw them to Israel. There are other Bible verses which use this type of language. For example, speaking to the King of Assyria, the LORD said, "I will put My hook in your nose, and My bridle in your lips."[217] God forced the Assyrians to return home in a manner akin to how they brutally treated their enemies. They would lead their captives by attaching cords to *hooks* in their jaws. Any movements to the left or to the right by the captives exacerbated the wounds in their mouths. There was no option but to go where directed. The phraseology of *hooks in the jaws* implies that the end-times invaders described by Ezekiel will feel compelled to proceed with their expansionist agenda to invade Israel.

The invaders will set their sights on the wealth for which Israel has worked hard.[218] Israel is a highly developed nation with vast resources. It is such a joy to see the Negev Desert wonderfully blooming with crops, trees, and flowers. Israel has

---

[216] Ezekiel 38:6,9 (see also page 128 for another perspective on these verses)
[217] 2 Kings 19:28
[218] Ezekiel 38:10-13

such expertise in desert cultivation that they run an agricultural school to train students from Africa and Asia in effective farming of arid areas. The Israelis have recently started producing natural gas from the massive *Leviathan* gas field in the Mediterranean Sea, between Israel and Cyprus. There are also chemical resources coming from the Dead Sea. This is the lowest point on the surface of the earth and the waters are so salty that people can float on its surface. There is a large industrial plant to the south-west of the Dead Sea which extracts valuable potash and magnesium chloride using evaporation ponds. There is much to attract a would-be invader who wants to extend and enrich his own empire.

The future desecration of the rebuilt temple will be a signal for the invaders to surge forward over Israel's borders, as described by Ezekiel. Their ultimate goal will be to capture the city of Jerusalem.[219] The Temple Mount in Jerusalem is regarded by Muslims as their third most holy site after Mecca and Medina. The sweeping through the land of Israel by *Gog* will be horrendous. Two-thirds of all those in the land will perish.[220] It would be disturbing for us to revisit the population figures given in Chapter two and to calculate two-thirds of Israel's current Jewish population. This will be "ethnic cleansing" of the beloved nation, not to mention the fate of the Jewish people in the *diaspora*. Israel's enemies are intent on wiping out the population so that they may be remembered no more.[221] Previous invaders of Israel such as the Assyrians, Babylonians, Greeks, Romans and Ottomans were cruel, especially the Assyrians, but was this ever their express purpose? Is it any

---

[219] Zechariah 14:2
[220] Zechariah 13:8
[221] From Psalm 87 which will be discussed in Chapter 14

wonder that the heart of the Lord is breaking as the times reach their fulfillment?[222]

I was lamenting this awful prospect with a Messianic minister from Israel some years ago. To my surprise, he commented that a salvation rate of one out of three in an evangelistic outreach is a good result. I was upset at the scale of the loss of life, whereas he was focussing on the precious salvation of the remnant of Israel. Looking back, I have to admit that he does have a point, and indeed this is the redemptive purpose of the *Time of Jacob's Trouble.*

Understanding the sheer extent and number of those who will lose their lives moves us to intercede for the salvation of the current population of Israel. We know that all the Israelis who die without faith in the One who takes away the sin of the world will sadly go to a lost eternity.[223] We want to pray for good ongoing opportunities for the Messianic Jews in Israel to share the Gospel. Compulsory military conscription gives young Messianic believers a natural platform to share their faith with fellow recruits from different segments of Israeli society. Like the Ultra-Orthodox, the Messianics are allowed time by the military at the start of the day for prayer and devotional reading. Pray for these young Messianic believers to be emboldened, strengthened, and protected.

On initial reading, these chapters in Ezekiel appear to talk about a very old-fashioned style of warfare. We read of the "army, horses and horsemen, all of them splendidly attired, a great company with buckler and shield, all of them wielding swords." God says, "I will strike your bow from your left hand

---

[222] Ephesians 1:10
[223] Matthew 8:12

and dash down your arrows from your right hand." We are told about the burning of the weapons after the war: "shields and bucklers, bows and arrows, war clubs and spears."[224] Ezekiel could only use terms with which he was familiar at the time of writing. The Hebrew word for horse, which is *soos*, means a leaper, and could cover something like a tank. The bows and arrows may refer to launched missiles, such as the rockets fired regularly into Israel from Gaza.

The account in Ezekiel of Israel cleaning up after the final battle against *Gog* removes any doubt that we are talking about modern warfare. It will take Israel seven years to burn the weapons of her enemies and seven months to bury the bodies of the invading army.[225] People will be employed full time to search for unburied bodies and bones, and will set a marker by the bones so that they will not be missed.[226] This description of cleansing the land is standard procedure for clearing up after nuclear or biological warfare.[227] Zechariah sets out what will befall the enemies of the Lord who come against Jerusalem: "their flesh will rot while they stand on their feet, and their eyes will rot in their sockets, and their tongue will rot in their mouth."[228] It may be that this is pointing to a neutron bomb deployed by Israel against the invaders. This weapon kills all living people and creatures within a certain radius, but has a less devastating effect on inanimate objects like weapons and buildings.

Many Jewish people in the *diaspora* (the dispersion of Jewish people outside the land of Israel) have family and friends

---

[224] Ezekiel 38:4,15; 39:3,9
[225] Ezekiel 39:9,12
[226] Ezekiel 39:14-15
[227] Warfare details from a talk on Ezekiel 38-39 by Chuck Missler, Koinonia House
[228] Zechariah 14:12

living in Israel. Recent media articles report Iran's claim to be "mapping" Jewish populations in the *diaspora* as a prelude to a murderous campaign should Israel attack its nuclear facilities.[229] Jewish people will be devastated when they become aware of the initial reports of Israel being overrun by her enemies. They themselves will face further and imminent great peril in the *diaspora*. We learn about how both Jewish and Christian people worldwide will fare during this time of the Great Tribulation: "Woe to the earth and the sea, because the devil has come down to you, having great wrath, knowing that he has only a short time." The short time will be three and a half years before Satan is captured. The woman here is the Jewish people, from whom Jesus came in the flesh. However, the persecution is not confined to them. We read "the dragon was enraged with the woman, and went off to make war with the rest of her children, who keep the commandments of God and hold to the testimony of Jesus."[230] This will also be a time of severe persecution of Christians by the Antichrist.

In Zechariah, it is not entirely clear whether the invaders from the surrounding nations are, at some point, joined by the other nations of the world. We see that the surrounding nations are the ones who initially lay siege to Judah and Jerusalem.[231] However, two chapters later, we read that the LORD "will gather all the nations against Jerusalem to battle."[232] There are two views on the implications of this. One interpretation is that other Scriptures clearly indicate that *all the nations* of the world will join the forces of the Antichrist in the battle

---

[229] Jewish Chronicle www.thejc.com: Iran 'mapping' Jews in diaspora for kill squads. David Rose. February 16th 2023

[230] Revelation 12:12-13,17

[231] Zechariah 12:2

[232] Zechariah 14:2

for Jerusalem. We read, for example, in Revelation that the kings of the *whole world* will be drawn to the battle, gathering in the assembly area of Megiddo.[233]

The alternative interpretation is that *all nations* is a further example of Middle Eastern hyperbole. A New Testament instance of this is the Roman census by Caesar Augustus.[234] This required Joseph to take his wife to Bethlehem where the Baby was to be born.[235] The Greek text speaks of the requirement of *all the world* to be registered. Common sense tells us that this was restricted to the Roman world, and indeed many modern translations reflect this understanding. There are numerous other incidences of hyperbole you will come across as you read the Old Testament.[236] According to this second interpretation, *all the nations* doing battle for Jerusalem are *all the nations* surrounding Israel which support the campaign of the Antichrist.

Various nations will object to the invasion of Israel. "Sheba and Dedan and the merchants of Tarshish with all its villages" will question the motives of the invaders.[237] *Sheba* and *Dedan* are areas in the Arabian Peninsula (in modern day Saudi Arabia). We are familiar with the account of the Queen of *Sheba's* visit to King Solomon.[238] Tarshish and her villages ('young lions' in some translations) may refer to the United Kingdom and her *lions*, or former *lions*, being from the British Commonwealth of Nations, such as Australia and Canada. Loosely speaking, it appears that nations which object to the

---

[233] Mike Bickle "Zechariah and the Battle for Jerusalem"; Revelation 16:14-16; 19:19
[234] Joel Richardson, Mid-East Beast pages 49-50
[235] Luke 2:1
[236] For example, Assyria is said to have made desolate (laid waste) *all the nations* and their lands; Isaiah 37:18
[237] Ezekiel 38:13
[238] 1 Kings 10

invasion by the Antichrist will be drawn from both the Anglo-sphere and Saudi Arabia. Bear this in mind when you read about candidates for Mystery Babylon[239] in Chapter 16 of this book. In these studies, we will continue to demarcate between Mystery Babylon and the Antichrist beast system.

Optimists today may say that Israel will never again be invaded because of the help which America will offer. This is not true, and God will permit a devastating invasion, suffering and captivity, because this is in His plan for the repentance and salvation of Israel. Various suggestions are put forward for the failure of the USA to adequately defend Israel. These theories range from America having an extreme left-wing government, to being decimated due to warfare or nature disasters. There may be readers who wonder if God would indeed allow such a fundamental weakening of the United States. The following passage of Scripture may be helpful: "For I am the LORD your God, The Holy One of Israel, your Savior; I have given Egypt as your ransom, Cush and Seba in exchange for you. Since you are precious in My sight, *since* you are honored and I love you, I will give *other* people in your place and *other* nations in exchange for your life."[240]

As we sadly witness the decline of the USA, our hearts must not only go out to America, but also to Israel, which will be left without support from the West. "Your broken *limb* is irreparable, and your wound is incurable. There is no one to plead your cause; *no* healing for *your* sore, no recovery for you. All your lovers have forgotten you, they do not seek you; for I

---

[239] World system with commercial aspects centred on Neom, Saudi Arabia or New York. see pages 143,144
[240] Isaiah 43:3-4

have wounded you with the wound of an enemy, with the punishment of a cruel one, because your wrongdoing is great, *and* your sins are numerous. Why do you cry out over your injury? Your pain is incurable. Because your wrongdoing is great *and* your sins are numerous, I have done these things to you."[241]

The purpose of God in the events of Ezekiel 38 and 39 is to be magnified in the eyes of Israel, "My holy name I will make known in the midst of My people Israel." "And the house of Israel will know that I am the LORD their God from that day onward." "I will not hide My face from them any longer, for I will have poured out My Spirit on the house of Israel, declares the Lord God."[242] This can only refer to a new relationship between God and Israel, based on their acceptance of Jesus, God's Messiah. We need to ask ourselves whether this has yet happened. Since this is not the case, sadly it must be that this invasion is part of the still-future process of the renewal of Israel, when they establish an everlasting relationship with the Lord.

The invasion of the Land is not something which those with a deep heart for Israel want to hear about. However, it is much better for Christians to understand these things in advance. This will prevent our faith in the Lord being shaken, as these events draw near and come to pass. We need to remain strong in the Lord, as Paul writes "my beloved brethren, be steadfast, immovable, always abounding in the work of the Lord, knowing that your toil is not in vain in the Lord."[243]

---

241 Jeremiah 30:12-15
242 Ezekiel 39:7,22
243 1 Corinthians 15:58

There are various prayer points that arise in this chapter. We may well find ourselves groaning in our spirit concerning the future invasion of the land of Israel. We know how certain world governments will react to the invasion, and can pray for leaders of other nations to join in the condemnation of the invaders. We can pray for practical support in the future for suffering Israel, both those who are Israelis and those in the *diaspora*. The foundation will be laid for this by the Church growing in an understanding of the practical implications of eschatology. We can be praying for our fellow believers to be prepared and strengthened for this task, ahead of this approaching time of testing.

| Jesus | *Yeshua* | יְשׁוּעַ |

10: Refugee Israel

"But the two wings of the great eagle were given to the woman, so that she could fly into the wilderness to her place, where she was nourished for a time and times and half a time, from the presence of the serpent." (Revelation 12:14)

Perhaps the most vivid picture we have of a refugee crisis in the Middle East is that of the Syrian refugees trudging on foot across Europe. Since 2011, over five-and-a-half million displaced Syrians have been forced to flee their country, escaping to places such as Lebanon, northern Iraq, Jordan, and Turkey. We may have seen the harrowing footage of children in flimsy summer clothes and insubstantial footwear, subject to wet, muddy, and wintery conditions in makeshift tent encampments. Families fled for their lives with what they were wearing or could carry with them. Turning to the *Time of Jacob's Trouble*, Jesus specifically asks us to pray that the flight of the believers from Jerusalem in the End Times will not be in the winter. We can assume therefore that the Israeli refugees will also be ill-prepared for cold weather.

We know that one-third of Israel will survive and be sorely tried.[244] Many will be displaced from their homes, perhaps taken away into captivity, or fleeing as refugees, or else hiding to defend their town or settlement. The Antichrist will set up his headquarters between the (Mediterranean) Sea and "the beautiful Holy Mountain" (Jerusalem).[245] This is of deep concern as the area includes Tel Aviv, the largest city in Israel, whose residents today total about 468,000.[246] It sits within the

---

[244] Zechariah 13:9
[245] Daniel 11:45
[246] Wikipedia "Tel Aviv" accessed 10th March 2023

Gush Dan conurbation, which holds over four million people, approximately 45% of Israel's population. Whilst we do not yet know which settlements in Israel will be overrun and how their inhabitants will fare, these geographical clues may help the church strategically to prepare to aid Israel in her hour of need. The *great eagle* referred to in the verse at the head of this chapter remains mysterious. Although the term suggests to some an airlift to Jordan, the distance between Jerusalem and Jordan is short and the terrain unsuitable for aircraft take offs and landings. The *great eagle* also brings to mind the USA but, as we discussed in the previous chapter, America is conspicuous by her absence in the end-times prophetic Scriptures.

There in the wilderness, the LORD will once again provide food and water for His beloved people, akin to how He provided for them during the years following the exodus from Egypt. This time, the provision will most likely be naturally administered through local believers, helped by overseas ministries. This amazing show of support may be supplemented by divine provision in the form of heavenly manna and water, drawn from the rocks, as in Israel's earlier wilderness wanderings.

The main destination of those in flight will be the famous red-rock city of Petra, which is situated in the south of modern Jordan in the Biblical area known as Edom. This ancient Nabatean city is the best fit for the place[247] prepared for the woman, owing to its geography. It is built into the side of sandstone cliffs and has an easily defendable narrow access passage between the rocks called the "Siq." Shortly before his death in 1935, the American evangelist Dr William Blackstone, who

---

[247] Revelation 12:14

was one of the founders of the Chicago Hebrew Mission,[248] arranged for copper boxes packed with Hebrew Bibles containing marked passages to be placed in Petra to instruct and minister to the future Jewish refugees.[249]

It has been estimated that Petra has in the past only housed up to 20,000 inhabitants, and therefore will be insufficient to accommodate all the Jewish people in flight from the Antichrist.[250] Some of the Israeli refugees will flee to Moab in modern-day western Jordan, north of Edom. Believers there are instructed to "hide the outcasts, do not betray the fugitive. Let the outcasts of Moab stay with you, be a hiding place to them from the destroyer."[251] This calling echoes that of Corrie Ten Boom's family, who bravely and sacrificially hid Jewish people in their home during the Holocaust in Holland. It is a mercy indeed (given their proximity to Israel) that Edom, Moab, and Ammon will escape the rule of the Antichrist.[252] The lands of these ancient peoples approximate to the state of Jordan today.

Jewish refugees will also be found in Egypt, where special cities will be set up to house them.[253] Hebrew will be spoken in five cities in the land of Egypt.[254] This will occur at the time of Egypt crying out to the LORD because of their oppressors. As a result, He will send to them a deliverer, who is Jesus the Saviour.[255] This oppression suggests that these five Hebrew-

---

[248] Subsequently known as the American Messianic Fellowship
[249] https://www.friendsofsabbath.org - History of the Place of Safety Doctrine in the Church of God By Craig M White
[250] escapeallthesethings.com – Is Petra the Prepared Place of Safety for Israel or You?
[251] Isaiah 16:3,4
[252] Daniel 11:41
[253] Isaiah 27:13; Discussed in Living Fully for the Fulfillment of Isaiah 19 by Tom Craig
[254] Isaiah 19:18
[255] Isaiah 19:20

speaking Egyptian cities will exist during the Tribulation rather than in the time of the Millennium which follows. There are Christians in Egypt already making preparations for Israel in the *Time of Jacob's Trouble*, including some even learning Hebrew. They would value our prayers.

Satan will be furious when the woman (Israel) flies into the wilderness, as portrayed in Revelation 12. We are told that he will send a flood after her. This suggests that the Antichrist will pursue some of the Israeli refugees with his army. However, encouragingly, we are also told: "But the earth helped the woman, and the earth opened its mouth and drank up the river which the dragon poured out of his mouth."[256] This opening up of the ground to devour the enemies of Israel reminds us of many incidents in the Old Testament, including the opening of the Red Sea and the drowning of the pursuing Egyptian army, when Moses led the children of Israel to freedom.[257]

The Old Testament gives us an example of supportive individuals providing for Israelites following escape from Jerusalem.[258] David's deceitful son Absalom stole the hearts of Israel in an act of rebellion. King David and his loyal men were forced to hide in the wilderness. Meanwhile, like the coming Antichrist, Absalom entered Jerusalem. During his flight, David was nourished by those who brought him and his men bread, raisins, fruit, and wine, besides donkeys for his household to ride. King David and his people had to endure a weary 21-mile journey from Jerusalem to the River Jordan. After crossing the river, David and his company went another 37 miles or so to Mahanaim, part of modern-day Jordan. When

---

[256] Revelation 12:15-17
[257] Exodus 14; see also Numbers 26:10 for the earth swallowing up Korah and family
[258] 2 Samuel 15:13 to 19:18

they finally arrived, local, loyal supporters brought provisions of "beds, basins, pottery, wheat, barley, flour, parched grain, beans, lentils, parched seeds, honey, curds, sheep, and cheese of the herd, for David and for the people who were with him, to eat; for they said, 'The people are hungry and weary and thirsty in the wilderness.'"[259] What an apt prefiguring of the woman, Israel, being nourished in the wilderness! Eventually, David returned to Jerusalem, just as Israel will one day also return there, after living as refugees in the wilderness among the Gentiles.

Some Israelis will also be imprisoned during the *Time of Jacob's Trouble.*[260] Jesus will rescue Jewish prisoners from captivity upon His return, saying "to those who are bound, 'Go Forth,' to those who are in darkness, 'Show yourselves.'"[261] This will take place during the time of "the day of vengeance of our God."[262] The LORD will rescue Israel for a *second* time: "Then it will happen on that day that the Lord will again recover the second time with His hand the remnant of His people who will remain, from Assyria, Egypt…and from the islands of the sea."[263] Assyria covered a massive swathe of the Middle East, and in this context may be referring to areas within Iraq, Lebanon, Cyprus and Iran. After the end of the final *week* of Daniel, the Gentile nations will bring the surviving Jewish people to Israel and will help to rebuild the devastated nation.[264]

---

[259] 2 Samuel 17:28,29
[260] Isaiah 42:22
[261] Isaiah 42:7, 49:9
[262] Isaiah 61:2
[263] Isaiah 11:11
[264] Isaiah 60:8-9

At the time the prophet Jeremiah was writing, Israel honoured God as being the One who miraculously enabled them to escape from slavery in Egypt. However, Jeremiah tells us that there will be a great change and, in the future, the LORD will be known as the One "who brought up the sons of Israel from the land of the north and from all the countries where He had banished them." "'Behold I am going to send for many fishermen," declares the LORD "and they will fish for them; and afterwards I will send for many hunters, and they will hunt them from every mountain and every hill and from the clefts of the rocks.'"[265] We look forward to Israel, as a renewed nation, being given a new spirit and honouring the Lord.[266] This did not happen on a national level following the founding of the State of Israel in 1948. This was merely a partial fulfilment of this prophecy.

Israel will be brought back by the Lord to inherit an everlasting righteousness. Jeremiah speaks of the latter days; the people of Israel who survive warfare and find grace in the wilderness will be drawn back to God to be His people.[267] Hosea writes, "Therefore, behold, I will allure her, bring her into the wilderness and speak kindly to her.[268] Just as the Lord will put *hooks in the jaws* of Israel's enemies to draw them to invade the land, so too will He exercise His sovereignty over circumstances to force many Israelis to flee to a nearby desert. In this sense, the Lord is *alluring* her into the wilderness. When God finally has His people's full attention there, He will speak plainly to them. This concept of God speaking to Israel in the wilderness is most interesting as the usual Hebrew word for

---

[265] Jeremiah 16:14-16
[266] Ezekiel 11:17-19
[267] Jeremiah 30:24 to 31:2
[268] Hosea 2:14-20

desert, *midbar*, is closely related to the verb, *to speak*. Luke tells us, "Jesus Himself would often slip away to the wilderness and pray."[269] Even today, Messianic Jewish leaders in Israel go into the wilderness when they seek to hear the voice of the Lord in a special way. Israel will yet embody the woman spoken of in the Song of Solomon, "who is this coming up from the wilderness leaning on her beloved?"[270]

This care for Israel will lead to an amazing relationship between Israel, Egypt, and Assyria during the Millennium.[271] "In that day there will be a highway from Egypt to Assyria, and the Assyrians will come into Egypt and the Egyptians into Assyria, and the Egyptians will worship with the Assyrians. In that day Israel will be the third party with Egypt and Assyria, a blessing in the midst of the earth, whom the LORD of hosts has blessed, saying, 'Blessed is Egypt My people, and Assyria the work of My hands, and Israel My inheritance.'"[272] At this time, the ancient rift in the family of Abraham will truly be healed. Hatred, warfare, and distrust will be replaced by harmony, unity, and a beautiful *shalom* peace. We can already rejoice over the pleasure that this eventual unity of brotherhood will give to the Lord. In the words of the psalmist, "Behold, how good and how pleasant it is for brothers to dwell together in unity!"[273]

Local believers, in the areas to which Israel will flee, need our prayers as they prepare and equip themselves for their crucial role. There will be need of financial support, shelter, water, nourishment, clothing, sanitation, education for the children

---

[269] Luke 5:16
[270] Song Solomon 8:5
[271] *Living Fully for the Fulfillment of Isaiah 19*, Tom Craig
[272] Isaiah 19:23-25
[273] Psalm 133:1

and medical care. Pray too for godly, wise, and brave leaders to emerge among each cluster of refugees.

Pray too for the State of Israel to be wise in making contingency plans in case of invasion. We need to be praying for men to arise in Israel, like the men of Issachar (Leah's fifth son), "men who understood the times, with knowledge of what Israel should do."[274] In 2018, the Prime Minister of Israel, Benjamin Netanyahu, employed a Messianic Jewish social media adviser. We can be praying for the Lord to raise up many such born-again believers into positions of influence in Israeli society. Think of the unpopularity of the prophet Jeremiah when he warned the people of Judah that they would be destroyed by Babylon. He was disparaged and betrayed by his own family. They hated his message that Judah should surrender to the Babylonians in order to save their lives.[275] He was beaten, arrested, put in stocks overnight, imprisoned in a dungeon, and ultimately lowered by ropes into the mire of an empty well.[276] His enemies wanted to kill him. We do not today expect Jewish people of influence, whether believers in the Messiah or not, to be abandoned in dungeons, but it is nevertheless always a daunting task to persuade the leaders of any country to make contingency plans for defeat. Those who speak up will doubtless face much pressure to be silent, and so will need our prayers for wisdom.

| peace | *shalom* | שָׁלוֹם |

---

[274] 1 Chronicles 12:32
[275] Jeremiah 21:9
[276] Jeremiah 11:21, 12:6, 20:1-3, 37:11-16

11: Armageddon

"For the LORD has a day of vengeance, a year of recompense for the cause of Zion." (Isaiah 34:8)

The *Time of Jacob's Trouble* comprises Israel's darkest hour: the sudden and violent invasion of the land, tragic loss of life, an ensuing refugee crisis and needless destruction of property. However, this is not the end of the story. All this awful suffering will culminate in the end-times battle for Jerusalem (commonly referred to as *Armageddon*). *Har* is the Hebrew word for *hill. Har Megiddo* is anglicised as *Armageddon*. It lies on the slopes of the Jezreel Valley, also known as the *Plain of Megiddo*. This final last days battle will be where the Lord will resolve, once and for all, the matter of who is entitled to the land of Israel.

We may well be asking ourselves why Israel, and in particular Jerusalem, is such a big deal to her enemies. Daniel tells us that the Antichrist will be infuriated by the *Holy Covenant.*[277] This refers to the promise of God to reward Abraham and his descendants, and to grant them a land in which to dwell.[278] The nations and people groups descended from Ishmael and Esau, excluded from this line, comprise a substantial portion of the hostile nations surrounding Israel today. The continuing resentment against the chosen line and their heritage will culminate in the *Time of Jacob's Trouble.*[279]

The seeds for this conflict are apparent from the Genesis account. God separately promised Ishmael's father and mother that the number of his descendants would be greatly

---

[277] Daniel 11:30
[278] Genesis 12:1-3; 15
[279] *Mid-East Beast*, Joel Richardson, ch.18 for a detailed discussion

multiplied.[280] Hagar was told that Ishmael "will be a wild donkey of a man, his hand will be against everyone and everyone's hand will be against him."[281] When Isaac was nearing the end of his life, instead of blessing Esau, his prophetic utterance was that Esau would live by the sword, and that he would become weary with serving his brother even to the point of conflict.[282]

We see this family tension continue throughout the Old Testament. In the Psalms, we read of the Edomites[283] egging on the Babylonians in their destruction of Jerusalem, saying, "Raze it, raze it to its very foundation."[284] Jeremiah recounts that the reason for God's judgement of Babylon was their gleeful, callous attitude when the LORD used them to discipline Israel and Judah. "Because you are glad, because you are jubilant, O you who pillage My heritage, because you skip about like a threshing heifer and neigh like stallions."[285] We learn from the book of Ezekiel that the LORD was very angry with certain nations because they enjoyed seeing Israel defeated. They clapped their hands, stamped their feet and rejoiced, out of hatred for Israel. The LORD attributes this to an ongoing animosity which we can trace all the way back to the time of Abraham, Isaac, and Jacob.[286] We read in Amos how the LORD will judge the nations surrounding Israel, because they "did not remember the covenant of brotherhood."[287]

---

[280] Genesis 17:19-20, 21:12-18
[281] Genesis 16:12
[282] Genesis 27:40
[283] Descendants of Esau; Genesis 36:8
[284] Psalm 137:7
[285] Jeremiah 50:11
[286] Ezekiel 25:6,15, 35:5
[287] Amos 1:9,11

This introduces another thread that runs through Scripture. The Lord uses pagan nations to discipline and punish Israel. He subsequently punishes these people groups for their malice towards Israel and for taking pleasure in their actions. God says (in Zechariah), "But I am very angry with the nations who are at ease; for while I was only a little angry, they furthered the disaster."[288] This speaks of the enemies of Israel having a vindictive attitude. The lesson here for us is that when the Lord prompts us to do or say something, we must be careful *how* we do it!

The prophet Isaiah encouraged the people of northern Israel who would dwell in the gloomy time of the Assyrian occupation.[289] He informed them that the Light of the World would be coming to this area of Galilee to illuminate their darkness and bring great joy. Isaiah prophesied that this Saviour will deliver Israel from her enemy. We are given details about the aftermath of this battle. "Every boot of the booted warrior in the battle tumult, and cloak rolled in blood, will be for burning, fuel for the fire." This brings to mind the account of the battle against the Antichrist in Ezekiel, when the weapons of the enemy will subsequently be burned as fuel in place of wood.[290]

God says in Ezekiel, "My fury will mount up in My anger. In My zeal and in My blazing wrath…" Chapter 39 of Ezekiel details how the Lord will defeat the enemies of Israel. Even the birds of prey and beasts of the field are invited to "eat flesh and drink blood."[291] John reiterates this point when he writes

---

[288] Zechariah 1:15
[289] Isaiah 9:1-5
[290] Ezekiel 39:9
[291] Ezekiel 38:18-19; 39:17-19; see also Zephaniah 2:1-3; 3:8

of the angel who cries out to the birds of prey, "Come, assemble for the great supper of God, so that you may eat the flesh of kings and the flesh of commanders and the flesh of mighty men and the flesh of horses and of those who sit on them and the flesh of all men, both free men and slaves, and small and great."[292] We naturally recoil from such graphic details but we cannot escape the fact that the Lord wants us to know what is on His heart concerning the defence of His people, Israel.

The waters of the River Euphrates will be dried up in the sixth bowl judgement. This will create a passage for the eastern military powers to join the other Gentile armies gathering at Armageddon in Israel.[293] Whilst we know that unclean spirits will ultimately draw the nations to *Armageddon*, nevertheless we cannot be sure why world leaders will decide to send their armies to Israel. Most likely, their intention will be to defeat the Antichrist's forces to gain control of his empire and the city of Jerusalem. All these Gentile armies will find themselves fighting against the Lord Jesus immediately after He returns to the Mount of Olives.

Zechariah provides many details of this final battle between Jesus and the Antichrist, together with the nations which have been drawn to Israel. Enemy horses will be blinded, and madness inflicted upon their riders.[294] The Lord will destroy the Antichrist with the breath of His mouth alone.[295] The final battle will be gory in nature. It will be "the great wine press of the wrath of God. And the wine press was trodden outside the city, and blood came out from the wine

---

[292] Revelation 19:17-18
[293] Revelation 16:12-16
[294] Zechariah 12:4, 14:13
[295] 2 Thessalonians 2:8

press, up to the horses' bridles, for a distance of two hundred miles."[296] How can blood rise up to four feet high for 200 miles? Even a narrow channel of this size would be hard to fill with blood. We can look to parallel Scriptures for an explanation. The Lord will send flooding rain alongside the other judgements.[297] Great hailstones each weighing an equivalent of 75 to 100 pounds (34 to 45 kilos) will accompany the final earthquake. The water in each hailstone will quickly melt. These verses suggest a mingling of blood and water. In the book of Revelation, the angel of the waters gives the blunt reason for this judgement on the enemies of Israel. He tells us that "they poured out the blood of saints and prophets, and You have given them blood to drink. They deserve it."[298] Perry Stone presents a different view that the verse is indicating that the dead bodies of the armies of the world, including the two hundred million fighters from the East,[299] will be piled up to the height of the horse's bridle.[300]

Jesus will be returning to the earth, with His saints, to fight the enemies of Israel. The Apostle Paul confirms this Old Testament teaching when he speaks of God bringing with Him those who sleep in Jesus, and the coming of "our Lord Jesus with all His saints."[301] The armies of heaven, riding on white horses and wearing white linen garments, will follow Jesus.[302] One of the centres of the ensuing slaughter will be in Bozrah, the site of the ancient capital of Edom. Isaiah has a vision of Jesus coming to Jerusalem, and he asks, "Who is this who

[296] Revelation 14:17-20
[297] Ezekiel 38:22
[298] Revelation 16:6
[299] Revelation 9:16
[300] Blood Unto the Horse Bridles. Perry Stone. YouTube video
[301] Zechariah 14:5; 1 Thessalonians 3:13, 4:14; See also Jude 14
[302] Revelation 19:11-14

comes from Edom?" Isaiah asks why the Lord's garments are red, and records the reply, "I have trodden the wine trough alone, and from the peoples there was no man with Me. I also trod them in My anger and trampled them in My wrath; and their lifeblood is sprinkled on My garments..."[303]

We may question why our loving Heavenly Father would act in such a drastic manner. We should remember that one of His titles is *Ish Milkhamah* (Man of war).[304] Another of His names is *Jehovah Tsva'ot*, which means *Lord of the armies of heaven* or *hosts*. God is a military commander, "The LORD of hosts is mustering the army for battle."[305]

We have undoubtedly moved into the arena of what is distasteful and even *offensive*. The Biblical doctrine of heaven and hell is similarly *offensive* to many, yet we believe it to be true as followers of Jesus. Our confidence in truth is unrelated to how much we like what we hear. This reminds us of the experience of the Apostle John, the writer of Revelation. He took the small book out of the angel's hand and ate it. At first, he enjoyed the taste which was as sweet as honey. However, during digestion, it made his stomach bitter, just as the angel had warned him.[306] We too rejoiced at first to hear the saving message of the Gospel. We may likewise initially be excited at the prospect of the Second Coming. These truths are like honey in the mouth to the believer's soul. However, eating is only the first part of the process. We need to let these matters sink deep into our souls, however unpalatable that may be. It does not take us long to painfully ponder on the awful future of all who

---

[303] Isaiah 63:1-3
[304] Exodus 15:3
[305] Isaiah 13:4
[306] Revelation 10:8-10

do not respond to Christ. As we engage more with the Bible's presentation of the End Times, we find that this too paints a very uncomfortable picture.

God will use affliction to purify Israel, "I will bring the third part through the fire, refine them as silver is refined... They will call on My name, and I will answer them; I will say, 'They are My people' and they will say 'the LORD is my God.'" They will be granted by the Lord "the Spirit of grace and of supplication, so that they will look on Me whom they have pierced; and they will mourn for Him, as one mourns for an only son."[307] The surviving one-third will mourn in bitterness, regretting the nation's blindness and hatred for the very name of Jesus, and the persecution of their brethren who own His name. This will be at last the salvation of *all Israel* that the Apostle Paul describes in his writing "and so all Israel will be saved."[308] "Jacob will rejoice, Israel will be glad."[309] The prophetic cry of David will finally come to pass, but at a great price.

Megiddo	מְגִדּוֹ

[307] Zechariah 12:10 to 13:9
[308] Romans 11:26
[309] Psalm 14:7

12: Preparation for Childbirth

"For we know that the whole creation groans and suffers the pains of childbirth together until now. And not only this, but also we ourselves groan within ourselves, waiting eagerly for our adoption as sons, the redemption of our body." (Romans 8:22-23)

The Biblical description of the End Times is characterised by the language of childbirth. During a mother's labour, as the time to deliver her baby draws near, her contractions become stronger and closer together until, at the height of her suffering, new life comes forth. We learn more about the nature of these eschatological birth pangs in the Gospels.[310] We read of false messiahs, war and rumours of war, earthquakes, famines, pestilences, and the sea roaring. As the time of the Lord's return draws near, earthquakes will become more frequent and powerful like labour pains. Tsunamis are caused by earthquakes under the sea, and so this fits with the concept of the sea roaring. If current international unrest and war escalates, earthquakes and tsunamis could be triggered by modern subterranean weapons. At the time of writing the second edition of this book, the situation between Russia and Ukraine could yet trigger World War III. This could even involve nuclear or emerging electromagnetic weapons of war. Modern warfare in our technological age is likely to include state-sponsored cyber-attacks that paralyse the internet, crippling critical infrastructure for essential utilities such as water, electricity and gas.

We should not let the significance of preliminary birth pains such as pandemics, inflation and wars pass us by. Jeremiah warned his readers that they need to gather strength as situations become worse. "If you have run with footmen and

---

[310] Luke 21:7-25

they have tired you out, then how can you compete with horses?"[311] We must prepare both ourselves and those around us for times to become increasingly tough. It is inevitable that troubles like the Covid-19 pandemic will cause many to question their personal faith. We owe it to our young people to teach them about what is ahead, lest their love grows cold through disillusionment. As difficulties deepen and life becomes more challenging, we want to see those in our churches prepared to dig ever deeper into the word of God and invest yet more in their relationship with the Lord. We want to be like King David who "made ample preparations before his death" for his son Solomon to build the temple.[312] We need to consider the words of Jesus, "but the one who endures to the end, he will be saved."[313]

This also reminds us of the parable of the wise and foolish virgins.[314] Each of the ten virgins had a lamp in preparation for the arrival of the bridegroom, but only five of them obtained supplies of the oil needed to light it. The lamps symbolise the Word of God, "Your word is a lamp to my feet and a light to my path."[315] We understand that oil is a symbol for the Holy Spirit, since it was used in Biblical times for the purpose of anointing, and we are told that Jesus was anointed with the Holy Spirit.[316] The parable of the ten virgins is a warning to us not to be content with mere intellectual assent to the Biblical doctrine of the return of Jesus. We also need the illumination and empowering of the Holy Spirit. Let us be among the wise,

---

[311] Jeremiah 12:5
[312] 1 Chronicles 22:5
[313] Matthew 24:13
[314] Matthew 25:1-13
[315] Psalm 119:105
[316] Luke 4:18; Acts 10:38

and so choose to go on being filled with the Holy Spirit, even while the birth pains are intensifying, and the Bridegroom is apparently delayed. We do not want to be among the foolish group, who are distracted and quench the Holy Spirit in their lives. Learning about the End Times and humbly preparing for the return of the Lord Jesus is an opportunity to prayerfully examine our hearts and our priorities. We must treasure our personal relationship with the Lord and so ensure that we regularly approach Him to be filled with oil for our lamps.

We will not be able to face what is ahead without the infilling and strengthening of the Spirit of God. As the days ahead darken, and the contractions become closer together and more painful, the love of many will grow cold. Therefore, it is essential that we learn today how to be ready for the return of the Lord Jesus, before it is too late.[317] The early, uncomfortable *contractions* serve this function in our spiritual lives. We are familiar with the *seven years* of plenty in Egypt, which Joseph used to prepare for the *seven lean years* of famine. The final *seven years* of this age, like the lean cattle, will also be ugly and gaunt. We are told that in the good years, Joseph gathered up an immeasurable amount of grain.[318] We should likewise prepare for the coming difficult days by building ourselves up with solid Biblical teaching, before we encounter "a famine…for hearing the words of the LORD."[319]

There are many other verses making use of this language of childbirth. Isaiah speaks of men's hearts melting and fear gripping them like a woman in *childbirth*.[320] Isaiah depicts the

---

317 Matthew 24:12, 25:11-13
318 Genesis 41:49
319 Amos 8:11
320 Isaiah 13:6-8

nation in times of chastening as a labouring woman.[321] He likens the rebirth of Israel to a baby boy being born and speaks of the time for the Lord Jesus to re-establish His kingdom, "shall I who gives delivery shut the womb? says your God."[322] In the Olivet Discourse, Jesus is using the image of a woman labouring in childbirth when He refers to the beginnings of sorrows.[323] Paul also uses this language in the context of the approaching *Time of Jacob's Trouble* when he talks about sudden destruction coming upon men just like labour pains.[324] The process of childbirth is relentless, intense, and irreversible. We should not be surprised if this perspective affects the nature of our intercession, as we are caught up in the magnitude of what we praying about.

When we see these labour pains intensify, we have a choice. The Lord tells us that when these things start to happen, we should stand upright and look heavenward because the time of being rescued by Jesus is coming close.[325] If we fail to do this, then we will be like those who love this life, for whom the intensifying labour pains[326] will be more like death throes, as worldly dreams and aspirations are smashed and reluctantly relinquished. This is a natural reaction, especially for hard-working people with a comfortable life, and goals to achieve. James touches on this when he tells the wealthy to weep and howl because their riches will fail.[327] There is an irony and a lesson here. Those in the persecuted church are far more

---

[321] Isaiah 26:16-21
[322] Isaiah 66:7-9; Hosea 13:13
[323] Micah 5:3; Mark 13:8
[324] 1 Thessalonians 5:2-4
[325] Luke 21:28
[326] Matthew 24:7-9
[327] James 5:1-6

likely to raise their heads in relief that finally the Lord is returning. For those of us privileged to have the freedom to practice our faith and some choices in our lifestyle, we need to remember that the Apostle John tells us that this world and its lusts are passing away.[328] Understanding the End Times can help us break free from being too attached to the things of this world. The deeper these truths sink into our souls, the easier it will be for us to lift up our heads.

We need to strengthen our spirit, even as the contractions speed up and become stronger. The Lord is greater than all that is coming to the nations of this world. We read that the "nations rumble on like the rumbling of many waters, but He will rebuke them and they will flee far away, and be chased like chaff in the mountains before the wind."[329] Even as many are caught up in panic, we need to meditate upon the truth which Isaiah wrote of, "you are not to fear what they fear or be in dread of it. It is the LORD of hosts whom you should regard as holy. And He shall be your fear, and He shall be your dread."[330] The Word of God is full of admonitions not to fear but to trust the One who will be with us until the end of the age.[331] It is replete with examples of God protecting, nourishing and delivering His people, such as during the Exodus from Egypt. We know that "Jesus Christ is the same yesterday and today and forever."[332] In these last days, let us strengthen our hearts by meditating on such incidents in the Bible and applying these principles to our prayers for Israel and to our own situation.

---

[328] 1 John 2:17
[329] Isaiah 17:13
[330] Isaiah 8:12-13
[331] Matthew 28:20
[332] Hebrews 13:8

It is appropriate to end this chapter concerning childbirth with the sad subject of abortion in Israel. We need to keep praying for secular Israelis, who comprise around 70% of the country's population. Promiscuity leads to many unwanted pregnancies. In Israel, conceiving a baby outside marriage entitles the mother to request an abortion. It is permissible by Israeli law to abort a baby up until the 39th week of pregnancy.[333] It is estimated that 1.5 million children died in the Holocaust, yet some 2 million babies have been aborted in Israel since 1948.

Aborting a pregnancy and taking away the life of an unborn child sheds innocent blood. This is akin to the ancient Israelites sacrificing babies to *Molech* in the Hinnom Valley, on the outskirts of Jerusalem. Israel was specifically forbidden in Leviticus to offer their children to *Molech*.[334] They were warned that any man who burned his children to *Molech* would be stoned to death.[335] The ancient Israelites offered their young children to *Molech* in the hope of gaining prosperity. It is valuable to remember in prayer the hard work of Messianic anti-abortion ministries in Israel.

| child | *yeled* | יֶלֶד |

---

[333] The Times of Israel "How Israeli ultra-Orthodox Women have taken back their reproductive rights." Andrew Silow-Carroll. 6th January 2021
[334] Leviticus 18:21
[335] Leviticus 20:2

13: Israel – Genesis to the Gospels

"Now it shall be, if you diligently obey the LORD your God, being careful to do all His commandments which I command you today, the LORD your God will set you high above all the nations of the earth." (Deuteronomy 28:1)

You may have heard it said that to understand Israel, you need to first understand the person of Jacob. In his early life, Jacob did not meekly lean upon the Lord, and certainly not when he wrestled with God through the night for His blessing. When determined Jacob would not relent, God eventually put his thigh socket out of joint and so, ever afterwards, he walked with a limp. Jacob was duly blessed with a new name, Israel,[336] based on his struggle with God.

This prefigures what is ahead for Israel as a nation. She will yet turn to the Lord, but not before the forthcoming *Time of Jacob's Trouble*, which Daniel describes as "shattering the power of the holy people."[337] Jacob's people will then accept a fresh relationship with the LORD, leaning upon God rather than trusting in their Jewish descent, zeal for their religion, and their sense of self-sufficiency. They will cease from doing charitable deeds to prove their own goodness before God; they will instead embrace, through faith, the One who paid the price for their sin on the Cross.[338]

The blessings for obedience and curses for disobedience in Deuteronomy further prepare us for what Israel is facing.[339] The first 14 verses in this passage illustrate how the Lord longs

---

336 Israel means God's fighter (Keil and Delitzsch Biblical Commentary on OT)
337 Daniel 12:7
338 Romans 6:23, 10:3
339 Deuteronomy 28

to lavish His blessings on Israel. He yearns to crown His chosen people with honour, dignity and fruitfulness. The remaining 54 verses are a gruesome and horrifying account of the consequences of disobedience. We may wonder why the Lord expounds on the curses so much more extensively than upon the blessings.

What happened after Moses conveyed the blessings and the curses? Did Israel fail to listen? Did she have a heart of unbelief when she received these words? The words themselves are clear enough to be understood without excuse. They were also regularly heard. Moses commanded that the law be read out to all Israel at the Feast of Tabernacles every seven years.[340] You may have heard the expression, *there are none so deaf as those who will not hear.* Did Israel intentionally refuse to listen and take these words to heart? It brings to mind the verse, "But to this day whenever Moses is read, a veil lies over their heart."[341]

In the blessings, we see an Edenic scene akin to the Millennium. In the curses, an awful picture is presented which has been repeated throughout history, most recently in the Holocaust. It will culminate in the *Time of Jacob's Trouble.* Had Israel welcomed and obeyed her Messiah, she would have no need for suffering to humble her and thereby bring her to the fullness of her promised blessings. Take time to digest and even weep over this passage, as it helps us understand the heart of God towards Israel. Before condemning national Israel for her

---

340 Deuteronomy 31:10-11
341 2 Corinthians 3:15

failure to heed these blessings and curses, we should each examine our own responses to various personal challenges in the Word of God.

The LORD describes the people of Jacob as *stiff-necked* on four separate occasions in Deuteronomy.[342] This phrase speaks of a stubborn, unresponsive spirit, something by no means confined to Israel. We are all sinners who, by nature, fail to seek God.[343] Jewish people are not morally dissimilar to Gentiles, but differ in their unique calling and responsibilities towards God, as well as in respect to their future. We are aware of Israel's faults because their rise and fall is documented for our inspection and instruction. More is expected of the nation of Israel, because she is in a covenant relationship with God, and so bears a special responsibility to be holy.

In Biblical times, the term *stiff-necked* was used by farmers to describe an ox which refused to obey the command to turn in a certain direction. The first Christian martyr, Stephen, summed up Israel's condition in New Testament times, when he spoke to the High Priest and Sanhedrin, describing Israel as being *stiff-necked* and uncircumcised in heart and ears, like their fathers before them, always resisting the Holy Spirit.[344] God longs for Israel to yield to Him. He has a plan to win her back to Himself. This will include a period of deep distress for the chosen nation, the *Time of Jacob's Trouble*. Through the prophet Isaiah, God cries out, "I have spread out My hands all day long to a rebellious people."[345] Imagine the pain of Israel's Saviour, the Lord Jesus, when He hears the disrespectful term

---

[342] Deuteronomy 9:6, 9:13, 10:16, 31:27
[343] Romans 3:9-20
[344] Acts 7:51
[345] Isaiah 65:2; Romans 10:21

many of His beloved people use to refer to Him. Israelis tend not refer to Jesus as *Yeshua*, but rather as *Yeshu*. *Yeshua* is a shortened form of *Yehoshua* (Joshua), which means the *Lord is salvation*. *Yeshu*, however, is an acronym devised by the Orthodox and is even used generally by secular Israelis, many of whom are unaware of its meaning. It stands for *may his name and memory be blotted out*.

No doubt, we would like to think that we could choose a less harrowing path to bring Jewish people to the LORD. We have to trust the One who has disciplined Israel since her inception to know best how to deal with His people and to lead them to repentance. He is the One who instructs and chastens the nations.[346] God is all-knowing, and we can only tremble at His wisdom. He tells us, "My thoughts are not your thoughts."[347] He does as He wills with Israel. When Jeremiah visited the potter's house, he saw a spoiled vessel being refashioned into another. God spoke, "Can I not, O house of Israel, deal with you as this potter does?" and "Behold, like the clay in the potter's hand, so are you in My hand, O house of Israel."[348] God is working through His plan to hasten the day when Israel will say, "we are the clay, and You our potter."[349]

God's discipline is not always pleasant for us to experience as individuals, and yet afterwards "it yields the peaceable fruit of righteousness."[350] This same principle holds true on a national and global level. "For when the earth experiences Your judgments the inhabitants of the world learn righteousness."[351]

---

[346] Psalm 94:10
[347] Isaiah 55:8
[348] Jeremiah 18:6
[349] Isaiah 64:8
[350] Hebrews 12:11
[351] Isaiah 26:9

After the *Time of Jacob's Trouble*, instead of being *stiff necked*, Israel will be "a humble and lowly people, and they will take refuge in the name of the LORD. The remnant of Israel will do no wrong and tell no lies, nor will a deceitful tongue be found in their mouths."[352]

The LORD's relationship with Israel is best understood in the context of a close family. "For whom the LORD loves He reproves, even as a father corrects the son in whom he delights."[353] Jesus starts the Lord's prayer with the words, "Our Father who is in heaven."[354] The theme of God being a father to Israel is found in the Old Testament, if we search for it. In the book of Deuteronomy, Moses questions why Israel disrespected God's ways, calling them foolish and unwise and says, "is He not your Father?"[355] The LORD expresses His complaint against Israel in Isaiah, "sons I have reared and brought up, but they have revolted against Me."[356]

God laments that Israel broke His covenant with them, saying, "although I was a husband to them."[357] There is a hint of wistfulness here. God expresses something similar in the book of Ezekiel, "I have been hurt by their adulterous hearts which turned away from Me."[358] We read in Deuteronomy 24:1 about a man who "... takes a wife and marries her, and it happens that she finds no favor in his eyes because he has found some indecency in her, and he writes her a certificate of divorce and puts it in her hand and sends her out from his

---

[352] Zephaniah 3:12-13
[353] Proverbs 3:12
[354] Matthew 6:9
[355] Deuteronomy 32:6
[356] Isaiah 1:2
[357] Jeremiah 31:32
[358] Ezekiel 6:9

house." The One who hates divorce[359] eventually gave Israel her certificate of divorce for her adulteries and sent her away when the Assyrians invaded the Land and carried Israel away captive.[360] God's injured heart is depicted through the writings of Hosea. This prophet was commanded to marry a harlot. Gomer, his wife, remained a prostitute, even conceiving children in her immorality. Whilst deeply hurt by this, Hosea nevertheless remained loyal to her, purchasing her back out of harlotry.[361] This is a prophetic picture of how the LORD will rescue unfaithful Israel (illustrated by Gomer), so that she will not again turn to her adulterous lovers. As Gomer eventually came to her senses, so will Israel, saying, "I will go back to my first husband, for it was better for me then than now!"[362] Israel will gladly follow the Lord into the Millennium and will never again doubt how good it is to be faithfully wedded to Him.

We may be reminded to pray for Jacob's people as we read the parables in the New Testament. Look out for Israel, the audience directly addressed by Jesus. In one such parable, we see a father, the king, arranging a wedding for his son.[363] Those on the guest list were far more concerned with their daily business, to the point of abusing and even murdering the very people inviting them to the wedding. In the end, the king's anger was so fierce that he burned up their city. Most Jewish people have sadly rejected their invitation to trust in their Messiah. Tragically, just 40 years after Israel abandoned her Saviour to the cross, Jerusalem was burned up, just like the city in the parable. Gospel invitations have been issued to those whom

---

359 Malachi 2:16
360 Jeremiah 3:8-10, 2 Kings 17:5-7
361 Hosea 1:2-10, 2:4
362 Hosea 2:6-7
363 Matthew 22:1-14

His messengers have encountered on the highways: the Gentiles. So far, the response of the Jewish remnant to the Gospel is a token of the rich harvest of Jewish souls yet to come.

We are surely all familiar with the parable of the prodigal son.[364] The younger son demanded his inheritance while his father was still alive and went away to a distant country. He disrespected the one who had given him these precious resources by living a wild, prodigal (wasteful) lifestyle. He returned to his father when he realised that his servants ate a diet better than the pig food he longed to eat. There, the elder son can be compared to the Gentile church — those who have followed Jesus for a long time, since the days of the apostles. The younger son abused his father's kindness, yet his father never stopped loving him. Notice how the younger son was moved by being in desperate need after his friends forsook him, mirroring the coming *Time of Jacob's Trouble* for Israel. The prodigal son's father welcomed him back, "For this son of mine was dead and has come to life again; he was lost and has been found."[365] The Apostle Paul likewise describes the eventual salvation of Israel as "life from the dead."[366]

We must not be surprised if many in the Church, like the long-serving faithful elder brother, harbour resentment at the very prospect of the people of Israel being reconciled to their God. Even in the millennium, will some Gentiles forget that their spiritual riches have only been granted to them by God's grace and mercy? Paul instructs the Gentiles not to be arrogant towards Israel, "do not be conceited, but fear."[367] The warning

---

[364] Luke 15:11-15
[365] Luke 15:24
[366] Romans 11:15
[367] Romans 11:20

is clear, "See to it that no one comes short of the grace of God; that no root of bitterness springing up causes trouble, and by it many be defiled."[368] How will individual Gentiles in the nations feel when they realise that their nation's prosperity depends on a journey to Jerusalem to celebrate the Feast of Tabernacles (Booths)? "If the family of Egypt does not go up or enter, then no rain will fall on them; it will be the plague with which the LORD smites the nations who do not go up to celebrate the Feast of Booths."[369] Satan will be chained up in prison during the thousand years.[370] Yet the sinful nature of man continues despite the fact that Jesus will be physically present here on the earth. It will be too late for the errors of replacement and fulfillment theology to hold any water.[371]

Will this resentment fuel the futile final rebellion of the Gentiles who come against Jerusalem in the second war of Gog and Magog? "When the thousand years are completed, Satan will be released from his prison and will come out to deceive the nations which are in the four corners of the earth, Gog and Magog, to gather them together for the war; the number of them is like the sand of the seashore. And they came up on the broad plain of the earth and surrounded the camp of the saints and the beloved city, and fire came down from heaven and devoured them."[372]

| Jacob | Yaakov | יַעֲקֹב |

---

[368] Hebrews 12:15
[369] Zechariah 14:18
[370] Revelation 20:2
[371] Replacement theology holds that the Gentile Church has replaced Israel in entitlement to the Biblical blessings of God, leaving the curses for Israel. Fulfillment theology takes the view that Jesus has already fulfilled the promises for Israel.
[372] Revelation 20:7-9

14: Eschatology in the Psalms

"O sing to the LORD *a new song, for He has done wonderful things, His right hand and His holy arm have gained the victory for Him. The* LORD *has made known His salvation; He has revealed His righteousness in the sight of the nations."* (Psalm 98:1-2)

Much of the book of Psalms is easy for us to relate to, with many insights into the prayers and heart of the worshipper, the penitent, the thankful and the troubled believer. It is also an area of the Bible's *beautiful garden* where many prophetic treasures lay hidden, just below the surface. Psalm 98, for example, prophetically celebrates the victory of the LORD on behalf of Israel in the sight of the Gentile nations. We read of the resultant musical praise and worship. This scene will occur at the return of Jesus, when the LORD will be coming to "judge the world with righteousness and the peoples with equity."

We are considering a very delicate subject. Our generation recoils from warfare, bloodshed, and revenge. Praising the Lord for the eventual defeat of His enemies may not be something which comes naturally to us. There is a lesson provided in the book of Revelation which helps us to adjust to such a concept. We see there what will happen when Babylon is burned with fire and destroyed. There will be enormous *joy* in heaven.[373] The twenty-four elders, the four living creatures, and a great multitude will rejoice at the judgement of the *harlot* Babylon. They will give thanks to God for avenging the murder of His servants. It will be difficult for us to get to grips with the subject of Israel's future, if we are squeamish and sentimental.

---

[373] Revelation 19:1-6

God's perspective on Israel's conflict with her neighbours is described in Psalm 2. "Why are the nations in an uproar and the peoples devising a vain thing?" We read of the leaders of the nations conspiring against the LORD and against His Messiah (or Anointed One), saying, "let us tear their fetters apart, and cast away their cords from us!" The Psalm recounts the Father honouring the Son and promising to Him all the nations as His inheritance. The Son will obtain His legacy by breaking the nations with an iron rod and shattering them like pottery. God declares, "But as for Me, I have installed My King upon Zion, My holy mountain."[374] Psalm 2 advises, "O kings, show discernment; take warning, O judges of the earth...do homage to the Son, that He not become angry, and you perish in the way."[375] During these latter days, we must continue to obey the Biblical injunction to pray for our government and other leaders.[376] Pray for unsaved leaders in our world to heed their warning to seek reconciliation with God. If they are not following the Lord, our leaders hold the potential to harm or lead many astray. Christian leaders also need our prayers as they are a special target of the enemy. In the time of King David, his people cautioned him, "You should not go out; for if we indeed flee, they will not care about us; even if half of us die, they will not care about us. But you are worth ten thousand of us; therefore now it is better that you be ready to help us from the city."[377]

Psalm 110 is the most quoted Psalm in the New Testament despite being very short. One important reason is that, like Psalm 2, it gives us insight into the Trinity. We hear God the

---

374 Psalm 2:6
375 Psalm 2:10,12
376 1 Timothy 2:2
377 2 Samuel 18:3

Father speaking to God the Son, "The LORD says to my Lord: sit at My right hand until I make Your enemies a footstool for Your feet." Abba Father is promising His Son victory over His enemies. This defeat of God's enemies will be public, crushing and humiliating. The nature of the Son's role will be gory. He will execute the leaders of many countries, judge among the nations and fill them with piles of dead bodies. The Lord will "shatter kings in the day of His wrath."[378]

The disciples of Jesus understood Scriptures like Psalm 110. So, they asked Jesus, after His resurrection, if it was the time for Him to restore the nation state to Israel.[379] At that point in history, this would have meant militarily defeating the mighty Roman Empire. At the time, the disciples were ignorant of the mystery of the gap between the first 69 weeks of Daniel and the final week. This helps us to understand why the Jewish people failed to recognise Yeshua as their Messiah on the grounds that He did not fulfil their expectation of a victorious military leader.

Psalm 97 takes on a fresh perspective in light of our subject, with snapshots akin to scenes from the book of Revelation. We see the rejoicing of the communities of distant shores at the dramatic return of the Lord. "Fire goes before Him and burns up His adversaries round about."[380] We can visualise people's reaction to the massive earthquake[381] which will accompany the time of His return, "The earth saw and trembled." No one can ignore His Second Coming and His treatment of His enemies, "all the peoples have seen His glory."

---

[378] Psalm 110:5
[379] Acts 1:6
[380] Verse 3
[381] Jeremiah 4:24-26; Ezekiel 38:20; Revelation 16:17-18

"Zion heard this and was glad, And the daughters of Judah have rejoiced Because of Your judgments, O LORD."[382] The last verse of this Psalm is an entreaty to the LORD's people to rejoice in Him and to be thankful before Him. This praise expresses ransomed Israel's delight in her deliverance by the Messiah and the punishment of her enemies.

The prophetic writings of Asaph in Psalm 83 contain the chilling words of those who live close to Israel's borders, "Come, and let us wipe them out as a nation, that the name of Israel be remembered no more."[383] These enemies of Israel span a massive geographical area compared to the size of Israel. The children of Lot are Moab and Ammon, descended from Abraham's nephew Lot and his daughters.[384] Edom is another name for Esau.[385] The precise identity of ancient Assyria offering support to the Muslim nations is less clear. End Times teacher and author Joel Richardson points out that when the Psalm was written, Assyria merely comprised northern Iraq, south-east Turkey and north-east Syria.[386] Broadly speaking, those listed in the Psalm are descendants of Abraham's family.[387]

The enemies of Israel are always on the lookout for moments of weakness. One such example of this is the October 1973 sneak attack by Egypt and Syria, known as the Yom Kippur War. Israel was vulnerable, because on Yom Kippur Jewish people fast, go to the synagogue, and largely stay at

---

[382] Psalm 97:6,8
[383] Psalm 84:4
[384] Psalm 83:8; Genesis 11:27,31; 19:37-38
[385] Genesis 25:30
[386] Joel's Trumpet internet site "Which nations does Psalm 83 Really Include."
[387] Psalm 83:8

home.[388] It would be akin to attacking the United Kingdom on Christmas Day. As part of our role as prayerful watchmen, we need to make ourselves aware of both the Jewish calendar and events in Israel.

At the time of writing this second edition in 2023,[389] Israel has been experiencing mass street protests and civil unrest from those who object to Netanyahu's proposed judicial reforms. Even military and air force reservists have been refusing to turn up for duty. US President Joe Biden responded by saying that Netanyahu would not be invited to the White House in the near future. During Passover 2023, rockets were launched into Israel from Gaza, Lebanon and Syria.[390]

We are naturally upset by divisions and factions that open up within our own families. In the Old Testament, we are grieved to read of the children of Israel at war with one another.[391] It is a sad state of affairs in Israel that an existential threat is the only thing that unites the State. This too must deeply pain the Lord, who has engraved Israel on the palms of His hands.[392] If we watch and observe internal divisions within the Land, so do the enemies of Israel. Jesus warns us, "Where the body is, there also the vultures will be gathered."[393] We can expect the enemies of Israel listed in Psalm 83 to continue their attacks as they observe signs of weakness in Israel.

This Psalm refers to an event from the book of Judges, where Gideon killed Zebah and Zalmunna (kings of Midian,

---

[388] The children like to go out and ride bicycles on the deserted highways and roads.
[389] April 2023
[390] Amir Tsarfati Telegram channel April 2023
[391] 2 Samuel 2, 18:3, 1 Kings 15. 2 Chronicles 13
[392] Isaiah 49:16
[393] Matthew 17:37

in the north-west Arabian Peninsula) and removed the crescent ornaments from the necks of their camels.[394] This is seen by some as a prophetic picture of the eventual defeat of the Jihadist Islamic enemies of Israel.[395] Today, we recognise the crescent moon and star as symbols of Islam.

Psalm 83 is thought to encompass the various attacks on the State of Israel since her rebirth in 1948. In particular, it may pertain to an end-times confederation of overwhelmingly Muslim nations intent on obliterating Israel.[396] These hostile neighbours will almost certainly participate in the invasion to be led by Gog of Magog, since in addition to the nations listed by Ezekiel, the text also refers to "many peoples with you."[397] This will ultimately lead to the nations of the world being defeated at the Battle of Armageddon. However, we read that the Lord will take an entire year to judge Israel's enemies. It could be that this campaign by the Lord Jesus will start with Israel's immediate neighbours named in this Psalm, and end a year later when the rest of the nations are gathered for the Battle of Armageddon.[398] "For the LORD has a day of vengeance, a year of recompense for the cause of Zion."[399] The ultimate fulfillment of Psalm 83 will be when Israel's defeated enemies seek the face of the LORD, and recognise that He alone is "the Most High over all the earth."[400]

---

[394] Judges 7:25 to 8:21
[395] *Mid-East Beast*, Joel Richardson
[396] Gog and Magog Explained by Psalm 83 A New Revolutionary Theory. You Tube video by Nelson Walters
[397] Ezekiel 38:6,9 (see also page 84 for another perspective on these verses)
[398] Psalm 83 War: Israel's Next War Predicted. You Tube video by Nelson Walters.
[399] Isaiah 34:8
[400] verses 16 and 18

Islam has a well-defined eschatology which may shed light on the prophecies in the book of Revelation.[401] Muslims are expecting the coming of the Islamic Messiah, the *Mahdi,* a 12th descendant of Mohammed. The *Mahdi* is said to be held today in a very deep well by Allah, but will arise in the last seven years before the final judgement. The Islamic name for Jesus is *Isa,* and he is believed to be returning and explaining to the world that he did not really die, but had been taken alive into heaven, and that he never actually made the claim to be the Son of God. The expectation is that he will play a major role in the conversion of many non-Muslims to the Islamic faith. *Isa* will insist that non-Muslims worship the *Mahdi* by offering people the choice to either follow the *Mahdi* and take his mark, or else be killed. Islamic eschatology teaches that *Isa* will not only cause many to embrace the Islamic faith, but he also will defeat the one they regard as the false messiah — the *Dajjal.* This imposter is seen as the evil, deceptive Jewish Messiah and is often presented as being blind in one eye. The *Dajjal* will be killed by *Isa,* or the *Mahdi* (according to which tradition you consult).

The Psalms provide a helpful backdrop to the events taking place in various countries around the world during the *Time of Jacob's Trouble* when Satan will be enraged with Christians as well as with Jews. This rage may be expressed in different ways. Some secular people tend to blame God when things are tough, so angry mobs could target places of worship. There could additionally be similar attacks on churches and synagogues carried out by extremists pledging allegiance to the new *caliphate.* Psalm 74 speaks of terrible destruction and violation of the sanctuary of God. It describes a scene of all the places

---

[401] Revelation 11:7, 13:11-15. See Further Resources on page 158 for suggested reading

where people meet to worship God being burned up. Once again, the challenge for followers of Jesus will be the admonition not to stop "assembling together, as is the habit of some, but encouraging one another; and all the more as you see the day drawing near."[402] It is likely that, in the last days, Christians will return to the New Testament practice of meeting in private houses.[403]

Some[404] even see the Rapture in Psalm 47, "God has ascended with a shout, the LORD, with the sound of a trumpet."[405] Indeed, where the Bible records the ascension of Jesus,[406] there is no mention of a trumpet sound. Paul makes it clear that when the Lord arrives to take His people from the clouds upwards to heaven, it will be accompanied by the trumpet of God.[407] Elsewhere in this Psalm we read, "He subdues peoples under us and nations under our feet."[408] Like those in Noah's ark, could this also be speaking of believers being lifted up out of the earth to escape the wrath of God on the world below?[409] Indeed, while Noah and his family were raised up on the flood waters, God's judgement literally poured down on the earth. This theme of the last days being akin to the time of Noah runs consistently throughout New Testament eschatology, "For the coming of the Son of Man will be just like the days of Noah."[410]

---

[402] Hebrews 10:25
[403] Acts 2:46, 5:42
[404] The Rapture is Found in the Psalms – Nelson Walters Last Days Overcomers, Weekly Newsletter 28th March 2023
[405] Psalm 47:5
[406] Acts 1:9-12
[407] 1 Thessalonians 4:16,17
[408] Psalm 47:3
[409] see note 404
[410] Matthew 24:37

Rejoice as you read the words of Psalm 45:3-4, "Gird Your sword on Your thigh, O Mighty One, in Your splendour and Your majesty! And in Your majesty ride on victoriously." The One coming on the white horse[411] will not be coming to shed His precious blood, as at His first advent, but rather His robe will be dipped in blood. This will be the actual blood of His physical enemies, who are seeking to finally destroy Israel. The prayer of the martyrs will be answered, "How long, O Lord, holy and true, will You refrain from judging and avenging our blood?"[412]

The Lord Jesus will be the ultimate *Avenger of Blood*.[413] In the Old Testament, this individual was the closest male relative of a murder victim. His role was to execute the penalty demanded by the law by taking the life of the murderer of his relative. The context of Gideon slaying Zebah and Zalmunna was as the *Avenger of Blood* for his brothers, whom these Midianite kings had killed on Mount Tabor.[414] Jesus will be avenging the blood of His Jewish brethren and His martyred followers. Meditate on the triumphant words from the Psalms, "Who is the King of glory? The LORD strong and mighty, the LORD mighty in battle." "Who is this King of glory? The LORD of hosts, He is the King of glory."[415] He is "the Lion that is from the tribe of Judah"[416] coming to rescue and avenge His beleaguered people.

The Psalms emphasise that God lives on a holy mountain. David tells us that when he was fleeing from his son Absalom,

---

[411] Revelation 19:11-14
[412] Revelation 6:10
[413] Numbers 35:19-27; Deuteronomy 19:1-13
[414] Judges 8:18-22
[415] Psalm 24:8,10
[416] Revelation 5:5

he cried out to the LORD who answered him from His holy mountain.[417] David describes those who live in the same place as God, as those who dwell on His holy hill.[418] The sons of Korah rejoice, "Great is the LORD and greatly to be praised, in the city of our God, His holy mountain."[419] We know that mountains are important to God. He met with Moses face to face on Mount Sinai when the Ten Commandments were given.[420] Jesus went up on to a mountain to share the Beatitudes with His disciples.[421] He stayed all night on a mountain praying before choosing the twelve apostles.[422] Jesus took Peter, John and James up to a mountain to witness His transfiguration.[423] Jesus ascended into heaven from the Mount of Olives, to which He will return.[424] As we go on through these studies and consider God's eternal city, the New Jerusalem, we will be looking to God's holy mountain.

Psalms	*Tehilim*	תְּהִלִּים

---

417 Psalm 3:4
418 Psalm 15:1 (see also Psalm 68:15-16)
419 Psalm 48:1
420 Exodus 19 to 34
421 Matthew 5:1
422 Luke 6:12-16
423 Luke 9:27-36
424 Acts 1:9-12; Zechariah 14:4

15: Who are these?

"And I heard the number of those who were sealed, one hundred and forty-four thousand sealed from every tribe of the sons of Israel." (Revelation 7:4)

How our hearts would rejoice if we were given a vision of thousands upon thousands of Jewish men, assembled together, worshipping their Messiah in glorious unison. John was granted just such a vision when he saw the Lamb of God in heaven, accompanied by the 144,000 singing a new song before Him, which only they could learn.

Each of the 144,000 is sealed for protection from the coming judgements of God.[425] This is reminiscent of the sealing of the righteous in the vision given to Ezekiel during a time of judgement for Jerusalem, when the angels of the LORD were poised to kill men, women and children. Anyone who had sighed and lamented over the abominations carried out in the temple was marked on the forehead and spared.[426] The Hebrew word for *mark* is *tav*, the final letter of the alphabet, which in ancient times was written like a slanted cross. This brings to mind how, through faith in the atoning work of Jesus on the Cross, we are sealed with the Holy Spirit of promise for the day of redemption, protected from the wrath of God.[427]

We are told that the 144,000 are *firstfruits* to God and to the Messiah – the first harvest before the conversion of all surviving Israel. Salvation will remain on the Lord's heart during the tribulation to come. Immediately after the 144,000 are re-

---

[425] Revelation 7:3
[426] Ezekiel 9:1-11
[427] Ephesians 1:13, 4:30; 1 Thessalonians 5:9

ferred to in Revelation 14, we read of an angel "having an eternal gospel to preach to those who live on the earth, and to every nation and tribe and tongue and people."[428] The good news of salvation in Yeshua will go out to the whole world during the *Time of Jacob's Trouble*. Jesus taught that the "gospel of the kingdom shall be preached in the whole world as a testimony to all the nations, and then the end will come."[429]

The 144,000 will be very special men: honest, trustworthy individuals who do not lie.[430] Their accompanying moral purity suggests that they will be young males since the Orthodox marry early and many of the secular are prone to promiscuity. The marking out and protection of the 144,000 illustrates God's grace in drawing people to Himself.[431] Most of us have unsaved family members and friends, and we should also take heart from this teaching that God will sovereignly watch over certain individuals even during the apparent chaos of the time of His wrath.

The 144,000 pictured in Revelation are gathered from the 12 tribes of Israel, albeit with the tribe of Dan excluded.[432] The reason for this is that Joseph is counted twice. Once he is referred to as his elder son Manasseh and once as Joseph (meaning the remainder of Joseph, which is a reference to Ephraim, the younger son). Even when the time comes for the land to be divided between the tribes in the millennial kingdom, Ezekiel instructs us that "Joseph shall have two portions."[433]

---

[428] Revelation 14:3-6
[429] Matthew 24:14
[430] Revelation 14:4-5
[431] John 6:44
[432] Revelation 7:1-8, 14:1-5
[433] Ezekiel 47:13

The doctrine of the 144,000 is of particular interest to the Jehovah's Witnesses cult, whose non-Biblical doctrine leads them to believe that only 144,000 will go to heaven. Their doctrine teaches these will be given a spiritual body, whilst the remainder will be given a fleshly body and granted an eternity on earth.[434] There is even a small group of Jehovah's Witnesses in Israel, as well as Mormons, who we can remember in our prayers.[435]

The *two witnesses* will prophesy for three and a half years in the final week of Daniel.[436] During the period of their ministry, Jerusalem will be trampled down, and the temple area given over to the nations. This will be the final phase of the *Times of the Gentiles*. The *two witnesses* will have a striking appearance to our modern eyes; they will be "clothed in sackcloth." They are referred to as "the two olive trees and the two lampstands that stand before the Lord of the earth." Moses and Elijah are their most likely identities. Indeed, these two great men of God were observed by Peter, James and John talking to Jesus at the Transfiguration. That event provides us with a picture of how Jesus will look when He comes a second time.[437] Jesus permitted these three disciples to view the scene to fulfil His promise that, before they die, they would see Him coming in His kingdom.

The signs and wonders that the *two witnesses* will perform further suggest that they are Moses and Elijah. These include

---

[434] gotquestions.org "What do the Jehovah's Witnesses believe about the 144,000 and a heavenly/earthly hope."
[435] Number estimated to be 1,600 in 2018, according to haaretz.com, *A Rare Glimpse into the Insular World of Israeli Jehovah's Witnesses* Israeltoday.co.il "How many Messianic Jews actually live in Israel."
[436] Revelation 11:1-14
[437] Matthew 16:27 to 17:13

preventing the rain from falling, which is reminiscent of the prophet Elijah, whose earnest prayers resulted in a three-and-a-half-year drought that led to a great famine.[438] We can expect such famine again in the time of the *two witnesses*. We are further told that they "have power over the waters to turn them into blood, and to strike the earth with every plague, as often as they desire."[439] This reminds us of Moses and the plagues upon Egypt.[440]

The phrase "the two olive trees" refers to one of the visions given to Zechariah. He saw a golden lampstand with an olive tree on either side to supply it with oil. The trees were described by the prophet as "the two anointed ones who are standing by the Lord of the whole earth."[441] Olive trees can live for thousands of years and yet still be fruitful. Moses and Elijah, just like highly valued long-serving olive trees, will likewise faithfully serve the Lord when they return as the *two witnesses*. We can only speculate on their appearance because they do not seem to be in their final resurrection bodies. We are told that after their ministry is completed, they will be killed by the Antichrist. Their dead bodies will be left on the street in Jerusalem as an object of derision, before they are raptured up to heaven. However, the Apostle Paul tells us that the resurrected body "is sown a perishable *body,* it is raised an imperishable *body.*"[442] The account of their death implies that the bodies of the *two witnesses* are earthly rather than glorified and immortal.

---

[438] 1 Kings 17:1; Luke 4:25; James 5:17
[439] Revelation 11:6
[440] Exodus 7-12
[441] Zechariah 4:14
[442] 1 Corinthians 15:42

Elijah had a spectacular start to his ministry. During the famine of his time, ravens brought him bread and meat, and a poor widow fed him with her supplies of flour and oil which supernaturally lasted years. He won a devastating victory on Mount Carmel against the prophets of Baal, and subsequently executed them. Despite these miracles, Elijah fled from Jezebel after hearing of her murderous intentions. He prayed to the LORD to take his life. In his depressed state, he said that he was no better than his fathers.[443] Little did Elijah then know that he would speak with the Lord at the Transfiguration during the First Coming of the Messiah or, indeed, be sent back as one of the *two witnesses* prior to the Second Coming.

We see the same pattern in the earlier ministry of Moses. He had the privilege of leading the children of Israel out of slavery to the Promised Land.[444] When Moses struck the rock, he was punished by the LORD and denied the opportunity to accompany Israel into the land.[445] Despite this, Moses saw Jesus' glory in Israel during the Transfiguration and will witness for the Lord in Jerusalem, with Elijah, before the Second Coming. Moses and Elijah encourage us that, even when we feel depressed, inadequate or when we are being disciplined, we can trust that the Lord is gracious and still has a role for us to serve Him.

The *two witnesses* will minister at a time of mayhem in Jerusalem. Their ministry will coincide with the Antichrist setting up the "abomination of desolation" in the temple. He will defy the living God by ignoring the Biblical restrictions concerning access to the innermost parts of the holy temple. The Bible

---

[443] 1 Kings 18 to 19
[444] Exodus 4:10
[445] Deuteronomy 32:51-52

stipulates that only the Levitical priests may enter the Holy Place, which is the location of the golden lampstand, the altar of incense and the table of showbread.[446] The High Priest was the sole individual permitted to enter the Holy of Holies, and only once a year on the Day of Atonement.[447] In Chapter 3 we saw how the Antichrist will "take his seat in the temple of God, displaying himself as being God."[448] It is easy to picture the outrage of the devout temple priests and their frenzied, but futile, attempts to resist this desecration. The *abomination of desolation* referred to by Jesus,[449] may refer to the Antichrist sitting deep within the temple or to an object he will introduce to be worshipped. Some believe that this object will be the apocalyptic *image of the beast,* which will speak and cause those who do not worship it to be killed.[450]

The two witnesses will be hated; those around them will repeatedly try to harm them to silence their testimony and ministry. Anyone who attempts to destroy or injure them will himself be killed by the fire which will issue out of their mouths.[451] This is reminiscent of the ministry of Elijah who was able to pray down fire.[452] They will be blamed for the long drought and its effect on food production in the Middle East. Even the waters will turn to blood at their behest and so become unusable for drinking, cooking, agriculture, washing and bathing. This will cause untold misery to ordinary people.

---

446 Exodus 40:12-15
447 Hebrews 9:6-7
448 2 Thessalonians 2:3-4
449 Matthew 24:15 (references Daniel 9:27)
450 Revelation 13:15
451 Revelation 11:5
452 1 Kings 18:38; 2 Kings 1:10,12

The two witnesses will be taken up to heaven just before the great earthquake, the final bowl judgement, which will divide Jerusalem into three parts.[453] This will be the crescendo of the birth pangs, "... the mountains also will be thrown down, the steep pathways will collapse and every wall will fall to the ground."[454] God will use this earthquake to create a valley that will provide an escape route from the fighting for the remaining Jewish people left behind in Jerusalem.[455]

We can expect footage of the exploits of the two witnesses to be beamed around the world, at least to areas where internet services and electricity are still available. When they are finally killed, their deaths will be widely and enthusiastically celebrated: "those who dwell on the earth will rejoice over them and celebrate; and they will send gifts to one another, because these two prophets tormented those who dwell on the earth."[456] Today murder by terrorists of individuals in Israel is celebrated in Palestinian cities with cheering and by giving sweets to people in the streets.[457] This is a chilling precursor to what is ahead.

The two witnesses will provoke a strong reaction from the Antichrist. Pharaoh was furious when Moses appeared before him demanding that Israel be released from slavery, and so he repeatedly hardened his heart in response to the plagues upon Egypt. Jezebel was enraged when Elijah both called down fire from heaven and killed the prophets of Baal.[458] The reactions

---

[453] Revelation 16:17-21
[454] Ezekiel 38:20
[455] Zechariah 14:4-5
[456] Revelation 11:10-13
[457] Amir Tsarfati Telegram channel 8th April 2023
[458] 1 Kings 18:38, 19:2

of Pharaoh and Jezebel give us an insight into how the Antichrist will respond to these *two witnesses*. Through the ministry of the *two witnesses*, God will show that He is not pleased with the invaders, and that He has not forgotten about His people, Israel.

We can remind ourselves to pray for Jewish people each Easter, which is roughly the time of celebration of the Passover. At the special meal, called the *Seder*, a spare place is laid for the prophet Elijah because he is expected to return before the Messiah. This practice is based on the Scripture, "Behold, I am going to send you Elijah the prophet before the coming of the great and terrible day of the LORD."[459] Moses too plays a large role in the Passover meal and readings from the *Haggadah* (Jewish written guide to the evening), as the Jewish celebrants (usually members of a family) recline at the dining table, recounting the escape from slavery under Pharaoh and listing the ten plagues that befell Egypt.

Pray that the Jewish Passover celebrants increasingly see the significance of the blood which was daubed on the door posts when they were in Egypt to protect their households from the Angel of Death.

olive	*zayit*	זַיִת

---

459 Malachi 4:5

16: The Earth and the Sea

"Woe to the earth and the sea, because the devil has come down to you, having great wrath, knowing that he has only a short time." (Revelation 12:12)

This verse indicates that woe is coming both to Israel (the *earth*) and also to the nations of the rest of world (the *sea*). The Apostle John describes the Antichrist as "a beast coming up out of the sea, having ten horns and seven heads, and on his horns were ten diadems, and on his heads were blasphemous names."[460] The implication of him coming from the *sea* is that he emerges from the *sea* of the Gentile nations. The Bible frequently refers to the nations, outside the specific land or *earth* concerned, as being from the *sea*. Isaiah proclaims, "Alas, the uproar of many peoples who roar like the roaring of the seas."[461] We should therefore expect the Antichrist to come from a Gentile land, which fits with him arising as the *little horn* from the division of Turkey, as we considered in Chapter 7.

By contrast, the False Prophet is described as "another beast coming up out of the earth."[462] His role will be to force many to follow and worship the Antichrist. The origin of the False Prophet from the *earth* leads to speculation either that he will be Jewish or, at least, from the land within the borders of the current State of Israel. Indeed, Israel itself is sometimes referred to as *the earth*. In modern Hebrew, the term *Haaretz*, meaning the earth or land, is one of the names used for the land of Israel. There is even a daily newspaper in Israel called *Haaretz*.

---

[460] Revelation 13:1
[461] Isaiah 17:12
[462] Revelation 13:11

Revelation Chapter 17 introduces us to a vision of a wicked woman, clothed in purple and scarlet, "and on her forehead a name was written, a mystery, "BABYLON THE GREAT, THE MOTHER OF HARLOTS AND OF THE ABOMINATIONS OF THE EARTH."[463] We know that this *harlot* will be wealthy and will have great influence over the rest of the world, for "all the nations have drunk of the wine of the passion of her immorality, and the kings of the earth have committed acts of immorality with her, and the merchants of the earth have become rich by the wealth of her sensuality."[464] Not only will the *harlot* be wealthy and powerful, but she will be self-indulgent, enriched by slave labour and, shockingly, is even described as being drunk with the blood of the saints.[465]

I have come across some very interesting theories that *Babylon the Great* may refer to Saudi Arabia.[466] This leads to the possibility that the wine which intoxicates the world represents oil. In other words, the rest of the world may be turning a blind eye to issues like human rights abuses in Saudi Arabia because they rely on her oil. It could be that the commercial aspects[467] of *Babylon* will yet be fulfilled by the new international city Neom, which is currently being built in Saudi Arabia. Its spiritual aspects[468] may be expressed in the city of Mecca, the destination of the annual Islamic pilgrimage, the *Hajj*. This is a plausible theory, since Isaiah teaches us that when Babylon is

---

[463] Revelation 17:5
[464] Revelation 18:3
[465] Revelation 18:13
[466] *Mystery Babylon,* Joel Richardson; zionshope.org, David Rosenthal
[467] Revelation 18
[468] Revelation 17

destroyed, "It will never be inhabited or lived in from generation to generation, nor will the Arab pitch his tent there."[469]

In 2020, the United Arab Emirates, Bahrain, Sudan and
Morocco signed peace agreements with Israel. This has been
dubbed *The Abraham Accords*. Do not be thrown by the fact
that Sudan (sometimes referred to as *Ethiopia*) is also listed
among the invaders of Israel in Ezekiel 38. Remember that
Israel's enemies will yet betray a future peace agreement bro-
kered by the Antichrist. Other Arab League nations, including
Saudi Arabia, were initially expected to make their peace with
Israel, yet in March 2023 Saudi Arabia agreed to normalise
their diplomatic relationship with Iran.[470] Ultimately, we can
expect Saudi Arabia to protest when Israel is invaded, as discussed in Chapter 9. This unstable situation indicates a split in
the Middle East. In one camp, we have those Arab nations
which are befriending Israel, recognising Iran rather than Israel as the major threat to peace and security in the area. Then,
on the other hand, we see Iran intent on expanding its hold
over its neighbours and destroying Israel. Similarly, Turkey
continues to strengthen its influence on the Middle East. It
may be that the Antichrist will be hostile to the harlot because
she allows the international residents of *commercial Babylon* to
enjoy a non-Islamic lifestyle.

Another compelling theory[471] suggests that Mystery Babylon refers to interconnected worldwide governmental systems
(the great prostitute who sits on many waters),[472] established

---

[469] Isaiah 13:20
[470] BBC online news article 10th March 2023 "Iran and Saudi Arabia to renew ties after a
seven-year rift."
[471] How the United Nations Becomes the One World Government of Mystery Babylon.
You Tube. Nelson Walters
[472] Revelation 17:1

by global oligarchs, who deceive through *pharmakeia* (pharmaceuticals or sorcery), making use of international agencies such as the United Nations, the World Health Organisation and the World Economic Forum. "For your merchants were the great men of the earth, because all the nations were deceived by your sorcery."[473] We read that Mystery Babylon will be the mother of harlots or prostitutes.[474] The worship of idols is described in the Old Testament as harlotry.[475] In Leviticus 20:5, the LORD describes Israel's sin in offering children to Molech as "playing the harlot after Molech." So, we may expect Mystery Babylon to promote false religion and abortion. Additionally, Revelation 18:13 indicates that amongst the trading aspect of Mystery Babylon will be "slaves, and human lives." This brings to mind modern-day human trafficking. It is not just a vain academic exercise to suggest the identity of Mystery Babylon, because we are enjoined to "Come out of her, my people, so that you will not participate in her sins and receive *any* of her plagues."[476] Opinion is divided as to the location of the city. New York City comes to mind as it is the headquarters of the United Nations. However, as Joel Richardson points out in his book "Mystery Babylon," there is no desert around New York. Isaiah's prophecy that the Arab will no longer be able to pitch his tent there when Babylon is destroyed hardly fits with New York. Additionally, Revelation 18:19 refers to those witnessing the fiery destruction of the city throwing dust on their heads, which is itself a Middle Eastern custom. This, in turn, emphasises why Neom may be put forward as a candidate for the city to be burned. Mystery Babylon is indeed mysterious! Could it

---

[473] Revelation 18:23
[474] Revelation 17:5
[475] For example Judges 8:27,33
[476] Revelation 18:4

be that the city John sees actually represents a world economic system rather than a specific geographical conurbation?

In Revelation, we read that eventually the beast, the Antichrist, will turn on, burn and destroy *Babylon the Great*, "the ten horns which you saw, and the beast, these will hate the harlot and will make her desolate and naked, and will eat her flesh, and will burn her up with fire."[477] It is therefore a mistake to assume the individuals leading Mystery Babylon will include the Antichrist. The harlot woman starts by riding upon the beast.[478] John saw, "a woman sitting on a scarlet beast, full of blasphemous names, having seven heads and ten horns." This suggests that at first the *harlot* controls and makes use of the beast, before the latter turns on her in furious destruction, enabling the Antichrist empire to dominate.

The book of Revelation suggests that we would be wise to keep an eye on China too. Commentators are divided about the meaning of the army of two hundred million associated with the River Euphrates and the sixth trumpet judgement.[479] This may remind us of Daniel's prophecy that the Antichrist will be disturbed and infuriated by rumours or news "from the east."[480] Furthermore, we are told that the waters of the River Euphrates will be dried up to make way for the rulers *from the east* and their armies, when the sixth bowl is poured out.[481] All we can say for sure is that today China brutally persecutes its own Muslim communities such as the Uighurs. We shall have

---

[477] Revelation 17:16
[478] Revelation 17:3,7
[479] Revelation 9:16
[480] Daniel 11:44
[481] Revelation 16:12

to wait and see if this is setting the stage for an eventual conflict between the Antichrist and Communist China, both of whom would be vying for world domination.

We cannot leave the book of Revelation without considering the troubling matter of the *mark of the beast*. We read that the False Prophet will "cause all, the small and the great, and the rich and the poor, and the free men and their slaves to be given a mark on their right hand or on their forehead, and he provides that no one will be able to buy or to sell, except the one who has the mark..."[482] The exact mechanism of delivering this *mark* is yet unknown. In the lands to be controlled by the Antichrist, this technology can be expected to incorporate the requirement to worship him and take his mark. Prophecy commentators have for a long time been preparing Christians for a cashless society in which our bank accounts are linked to a microchip embedded in our bodies. The World Economic Forum's website goes even further in its analysis of "The Fourth Industrial Revolution." It speaks of our bodies becoming so enhanced by technology that there will be a blurring of the margin between our bodies and digital systems.[483] Central Bank Digital Currency (CBDC), supported by the sort of social credit system currently in use in China, may be creeping ever nearer. Most of us are oblivious to the potential ramifications of a centralised, programmable digital currency, where fines may be instantaneously deducted for breaches of the government's latest edicts, without any prior legal process.

What are the eternal implications of Christians taking the *mark of the beast*? Jesus says, "I give them eternal life, and they will never perish; and no one will snatch them out of My

---

[482] Revelation 13:16-17
[483] weforum.org, *The Fourth Industrial Revolution: what it means, how to respond*

hand."[484] "All that the Father gives Me will come to Me, and the one who comes to Me I will certainly not cast out."[485] However, these promises do not preclude us from deliberately walking away from "so great a salvation."[486] The warning in Scripture is clear for all to read and will, in the future, be reinforced by an angel declaring with a loud voice, "If anyone worships the beast and his image, and receives a mark on his forehead or on his hand, he also will drink of the wine of the wrath of God, which is mixed in full strength in the cup of His anger; and he will be tormented with fire and brimstone in the presence of the holy angels and in the presence of the Lamb ... they have no rest day and night, those who worship the beast and his image, and whoever receives the mark of his name."[487] Let us resolve not to sell our birthright for a bowl of potage.[488]

We are warned in the Bible, "Awake, sleeper and arise from the dead, and Christ will shine on you."[489] Paul encourages us, "But you, brethren, are not in darkness, that the day would overtake you like a thief; for you are all sons of light and sons of day…so then let us not sleep as others do, but let us be alert and sober."[490] These encroaching inroads into our very biological essence, ostensibly for our benefit, will be yet another deception of the End Times. This is a further indicator that Jesus must return very soon before future generations completely lose their God-created humanity. Indeed, Jesus tells us that "unless those days had been cut short, no life

---

[484] John 10:28
[485] John 6:37
[486] Hebrews 2:3 (see also Hebrews 6:1-8)
[487] Revelation 14:9-11
[488] Genesis 25:29-34
[489] Ephesians 5:14
[490] 1 Thessalonians 5:4-6

would have been saved; but for the sake of the elect those days will be cut short."[491]

Governments outside of the realm of the Antichrist can be expected to employ similar technology to control their people. Deception from those who govern us will thrive. There may be Christians who find it offensive to suggest that we need to prayerfully consider the messages spread by our governments and media outlets. Satan is the father of lies, and deceptions will not be confined to the religious realm.[492] We owe it to ourselves and our families to be prepared. We would be wise to fix the words of the Apostle Paul in our minds, "so that no advantage would be taken of us by Satan, for we are not ignorant of his schemes."[493] Never will discernment be more vital to the believer than in the last days. We truly need to be those "who because of practice have their senses trained to discern good and evil."[494]

We need to cry out to the Lord to awaken His church and to clothe us in wisdom and discernment, especially as His return draws nearer. As we observe evils rising around us, we can take heart from Jeremiah's observation that the reason we are not destroyed is because of the merciful, kind love (in Hebrew, *Hesed*) and compassion of the LORD.[495] Jesus embodies this *Hesed* love, and will again demonstrate it publicly, when He comes to rescue His people from the tyranny of evil.

loving kindness	*hesed*	חֶסֶד

---

[491] Matthew 24:22
[492] John 8:44
[493] 2 Corinthians 2:11
[494] Hebrews 5:14
[495] Lamentations 3:22

17: God's Judgements

"Then I saw when the Lamb broke one of the seven seals, and I heard one of the four living creatures saying as with a voice of thunder, "Come.""
(Revelation 6:1)

The prophet Daniel was divinely instructed to seal up the scroll of his writings until the time of the end. In the book of Revelation, the Apostle John likewise saw the Father on the throne of heaven holding another scroll written both on the inside and also on the back. This scroll was firmly secured with seven seals. The significance of this would have been clearly understood by the Apostle John. The seven seals and double-sided writing were characteristic of a special legal document prepared whenever land was sold in Biblical times. This entitled a willing, financially able and close male relative of the seller to later buy back (or redeem) the land within a certain period of time.[496] In Ruth 4, we see Boaz as the nearest willing relative (kinsman, *goel* in Hebrew) exercising his right to buy back land previously sold by Naomi's late husband Elimelech.

Scripture tells us that Satan is "the prince of the power of the air,"[497] and "the whole world lies in the power of the evil one."[498] As these last days darken, we can be in no doubt as to the truth of this doctrine, given how we experience this world's constant moral and spiritual assaults. We desperately need our world to be bought back from the enemy of our souls, and to be redeemed by our Kinsman Redeemer, the Lord Jesus

[496] Our Redeemer Kinsman and the Seven-Sealed Book Volume 8 a Book on Bible Prophecy by Ernest Angley, internet article.
Revelation Chapter 5:1-7 "Our Kinsman Redeemer" Calvary Chapel Fellowship of Enid Matthew W. Thoms, April 2017
[497] Ephesians 2:2
[498] 1 John 5:19

Christ, who is not ashamed to call us brothers.[499] This is the reason why, when Jesus takes the scroll in Revelation 5, the four living creatures and the 24 elders sang a new song celebrating how Jesus is worthy to unseal it, because He has redeemed us by His blood.[500] The process of our Kinsman Redeemer purchasing back the entire earth will be a painful one, since each seal He breaks open unleashes a fresh judgement. The seventh seal heralds the seven trumpet judgements. After this come the seven bowl judgements of the wrath of God.

"I looked, and behold, a black horse; and he who sat on it had a pair of scales in his hand."[501] This *black horse* suggests a time of great scarcity. There will be not be enough food in the world and ordinary people will not be able to afford to purchase what there is. The situation reminds us of the peak of the hyperinflation suffered by the Weimar Republic in 1923 and, in more recent years, in Venezuela. This sort of economic crisis will be repeated as we near the end of the age, triggered by various troubles ranging from pestilences to natural disasters and wars, presumably as governments borrow or simply print more and more money to finance their nations' responses. The super-rich elite, however, will be unaffected. Revelation emphasises the inequality, referring to the luxuries of the rich as the *oil and the wine*, "a quart of wheat for a denarius, and three quarts of barley for a denarius; and do not damage the oil and the wine."[502] A *denarius* was a typical day's wage of a labourer, as we see in the parable of the workers in the

---

[499] Hebrews 2:11
[500] Revelation 5:9
[501] Revelation 6:5
[502] Revelation 6:6

vineyard.[503] A quart (sufficient to almost fill a one litre container) of wheat or barley was considered sufficient food for one person for one day. This suggests that a day's wages could be spent on bread to feed just a single person or eked out to purchase cereal to feed three.

The breaking of the fourth seal ushers in the death of a quarter of the world's population through war, famine, pestilence, and wild animals. In the Western world, improvements in sanitation and living conditions have reduced infant mortality and increased life expectancy by preventing disease caused by common pathogens. It may therefore puzzle us why Jesus lists *pestilences* among the troubles in the End Times.[504] We can expect that the natural and man-made disasters in the last days will force people to live in makeshift public or emergency shelters and camps. Normal levels of sanitation and hygiene will not be possible in such a setting and outbreaks of illnesses like cholera and typhoid could easily spread. Then, there are virology research laboratories all over the world. We cannot dismiss the possibility of future accidental release (through earthquakes, for example), or even the deliberate spread, of killer viruses. These may have a higher mortality rate than the recent novel coronavirus and could be even more disruptive to our way of life. The prospect of further *pestilences* only emphasises the likelihood that the sorts of restrictions we saw during Covid-19 pandemic will form part of the picture of the last days. This, in turn, enhances the challenges of the New Testament exhortation to meet for Christian fellowship and encouragement as we see the day of the Lord's return approaching.[505]

---

[503] Matthew 20:1-16
[504] Matthew 24:7
[505] Hebrews 10:24-25

We must be prepared for meetings to be informal and off the radar of governing authorities.

There are many other dangers lurking in the world which may have to be endured during the time of the Great Tribulation, since Satan will be cast out of heaven with his angels to wreak havoc upon the earth.[506] The use of nuclear weapons, owned by many countries of the world, is yet another one of these potential disasters. We read of signs in the stars which are likely to refer to meteorite strikes. Already NASA is tracking a huge asteroid headed in our direction. It has been named *Apophis*. This is reported to be passing close to our planet in 2029, before returning seven years later when it is more likely to hit the earth.[507] Jesus also speaks of there being signs in the sun.[508] These *signs* may well also include another solar storm like the Carrington Storm of 1859. This caused electrons to surge through telegraph wires, giving strong electric shocks to telegraph operators and causing fires. We are nowadays much more reliant on the electric grid and modern telecommunications, both for daily living and for the maintenance of our supply chains. The *birth pangs of the Messiah* (as the Talmud describes such signs) will be like childbirth: painful, messy, noisy, and undignified.

During the fourth seal, "the wild beasts of the earth" will kill people. We may ponder how this could possibly come to pass. In February 2021, there were reports of growing numbers of abandoned hippos in Columbia, which scientists fear

[506] Revelation 12:7-10
[507] thenorthernecho.co.uk, *Giant asteroid Apophis heading for the earth in 2029 says NASA*
[508] Luke 21:25

will eventually attack humans.[509] During March 2021, Australia was hit by a plague of rodents endangering drinking water and even biting three hospital patients.[510] These sorts of problems can be expected to escalate in the world during the upheaval of the last days and the *Time of Jacob's Trouble*. It is also possible that when Satan is thrown down from heaven with a third of his angels,[511] some of these demonic creatures will go on to possess animals and thereby inflict great physical harm to humans through them. A different suggestion from Perry Stone is that this reference to animals may allude to biological weapons based on the development of animal viruses.

The trumpet and bowl judgements comprise the outpouring of the wrath of God. Even in His wrath, God shows mercy. For example, the fifth trumpet, being a plague of demonic locusts, only affects those who are not sealed, being those who have not yet at this point repented of their sins and put their trust in the Lord. Repentance and salvation are still options in this most terrible time upon the earth. The trumpets are by-and-large judgements of thirds. We see one-third of trees burned, one-third of the sea turned to blood, one-third of fish dying, one-third of fresh waters being made bitter, and one-third of celestial bodies darkened. The sixth trumpet judgement kills one-third of mankind, which we can assume refers to a third of the three-quarters who remain after the seal judgements.[512] A simple calculation shows that the combination of the fourth seal and the sixth trumpet judgements could

[509] dailymail.co.uk/news/article-7953393/Pablo-Escobars-hippos-causing-environmental-nightmare-Colombia.html, *Mail Online*, 4th February 2021
[510] dailymail.co.uk/news/article-9378677/Three-hospital-patients-bitten-MICE-amid-New-South-Wales-rodent-plague.html, *Mail Online*, 19th March 2021
[511] Revelation 12:3,4,9
[512] Revelation 6:8, 9:15,18

result in a reduction of 50% in the world's population.[513] It would be a grave mistake to think of Israel going through deep tribulation while the rest of the world is relatively undisturbed.

The trumpet judgements are followed by the seven bowl (or *vial*) judgements. Once again God shows mercy. The first bowl judgement of sores only affects the "unsealed." However, we are no longer restricted to one-thirds. All the unsealed who have the *mark of the beast* and who worship the *image of the beast* are afflicted with sores, all the living creatures in the sea perish, all the fresh water turns to blood and in the seventh bowl, "every island fled, and no mountains were found."[514]

In Old Testament times, Amos described Israel's sin and God's judgement. Amos pointed five times to God's disappointment at Israel's lack of repentance, "Yet you have not returned to Me."[515] This shows us the heart of our loving Heavenly Father in sending judgement. He is seeking a repentant response to the discipline He sends our way. Eventually, we see in Amos that when enough was enough, God declared, "Prepare to meet your God, O Israel." In the same way, the LORD will give an opportunity for those who have resisted taking the *mark of the beast* to turn to Him and repent of their sins. Once again, there will be a limit to His patience, and the time will yet come when God will pour out His wrath in the world during the trumpet and bowl judgements. However, even at the very end, the way will remain open for salvation to those who are still free of the Antichrist's seal of perdition. We read in the book of Joel that even while the sun is being turned to darkness, and the moon to blood, even when there will be

---

[513] See Isaiah 13:12; 24:6
[514] Revelation 16:20
[515] Amos 4

obvious signs on earth, such as blood, fire and smoke, even then, whoever calls on the name of the LORD will be saved.[516]

How long will the wrath of God last? Nelson Walters comments that Noah was in the ark for one year and ten days: from the 17th day of the second month until the 27th day of the same month in the following year.[517] This was the period of time that Noah and his family were lifted up in the ark (a type of the Rapture), above the judgement taking place below. Since we are told that the last days will be "as in the days of Noah,"[518] he suggests that this will also be how long the wrath of God will be poured out following the Rapture. This exactly fits in with the period between *Rosh HaShanah* of one year and *Yom Kippur* of the following year, as discussed in Chapter 5.

During the trumpet and bowl judgements, the Lord, our Creator, will be showing what He thinks about the arrogance and sin of mankind. Society has shown contempt for life, not only through accepting the abomination of abortion, but also through such practices as euthanasia and savage end-of-life medical protocols. We hear of scientists working on geoengineering and ways to block the sun (such as atmospheric particle spraying) using the excuse of climate change, notably global warming.[519] Our seas and waterways are polluted with various chemicals and plastics. In the description of the wrath of God,

---

[516] Joel 2:30-32, Acts 2:17-21
[517] You tube video: Noah's Flood and End Time Prophecy. Genesis 7:11; 8:14-20
[518] Matthew 24:37-39, see also page 130
[519] https://www.forbes.com Solar Geoengineering: Why Bill Gates Wants It, But These Experts Want To Stop It

men seek death but it escapes them;[520] the sun scorches mankind;[521] the sea and fresh waters becomes blood; and every living sea creature dies.[522] After the fierceness of the sun in the fourth bowl, darkness will envelop the kingdom of the beast.[523] God is the One who controls the power of the sun, not mankind.

The trumpet and bowl judgement bring to mind the 10 plagues upon Egypt in the time of Moses, which Jewish people remember at Passover. We read in Revelation of hail, blood, polluted water, dead fish, darkness, sores, demonic frogs and locusts, and death.[524] Just as Pharoah and the Egyptians hardened their hearts,[525] so too many will harden their hearts during these awful judgements.[526] The events surrounding the national conversion of Israel at the final week of Daniel will be a further fulfillment of Passover. We are specifically told that the Israelites dwelling in Goshen were spared the plagues of flies, cattle death, darkness and hail.[527] It is therefore likely that the Israelis left in the Land, and those taking refuge in such places as Petra and the five cities in Egypt, will also be spared. However, instead of Moses subsequently leading them back to the Promised Land, this time that role will be ultimately fulfilled by the Lord Jesus, as we looked at in the Chapter "Refugee Israel."

---

[520] Revelation 9:6
[521] Revelation 16:8,9
[522] Revelation 16:3-6
[523] Revelation 16:10
[524] Exodus 7:17-21; 8 :6 ; 9:9-11,23 ; 10 :2,12-15
[525] Exodus 14:17, 1 Samuel 6:6
[526] Revelation 16:11
[527] Exodus 8:22; 9:4,26; 10:23

It is a solemn subject to consider the predicament of the few survivors of the 70th *week* of Daniel. The prophet Isaiah graphically describes the scene of the great earthquake in the End Times, and the brightness of the coming of the LORD of Hosts.[528] He writes of a picture so bleak that it matches any Hollywood disaster movie. Isaiah speaks of drastic geological changes to the surface of the earth, land being emptied and plundered, houses shut up, misery, destruction, and global desolation. Chapters 24 to 27 of his prophecy are often referred to as the "Apocalypse of Isaiah."

There is another reference to this mighty end-of-age earthquake in the description of the seventh bowl judgement.[529] We read "there was a great earthquake, such as there had not been since man came to be upon the earth..." It will divide Jerusalem into three parts and cause the cities of the nations to fall. Ezekiel describes how "the fish of the sea, the birds of the heavens, the beasts of the field, all the creeping things that creep on the earth, and all the men who are on the face of the earth" will shake at the presence of God. The passage continues "the mountains also will be thrown down, the steep pathways will collapse and every wall will fall to the ground."[530]

It is likely that this massive earthquake will occur at the moment that Jesus' feet touch the Mount of Olives. "In that day His feet will stand on the Mount of Olives," which will split in two "from east to west by a very large valley."[531] The resulting geological upheaval will pave the way for the renewed earth during the Millennium. We can only ponder in horror

---

[528] Isaiah 24:19-23
[529] Revelation 16:17-21
[530] Ezekiel 38:19-20
[531] Zechariah 14:4

the consequences of the devastation upon structures like nuclear power stations, military weapon stores, oil refineries, and chemical factories.

God will judge humanity in three distinct and ultimate judgements. The first is the *Bema*, which is the Greek translation of *judgement seat*.[532] The term alludes to a raised stage in Ancient Greece, where winners of athletic competitions were given crowns as prizes. We are warned "for we will all stand before the judgment seat of God."[533] This *Bema* judgement is just for Christians, to receive rewards for our service to the Lord, based on the degree of our faithfulness.

What we have done for the Lord will be revealed: "gold, silver, precious stones, wood, hay, straw, each man's work will become evident; for the day will show it because it is to be revealed with fire, and the fire itself will test the quality of each man's work." This is the reason why Paul instructs us to be careful how we build in our lives.[534] In the same epistle, he tells us that all things are lawful for us but not all things are profitable.[535] This is said in the context of us not being enslaved or controlled by any habit and being unselfish. We can also reflect that these unprofitable behaviours will be classified at the Bema judgement as *wood, hay, and straw*.

Life is short and its pleasures fleeting. We only have a very limited time to build up our treasure in heaven, which will last for all eternity. We may have heard the phrase that when believers die, they have been *promoted to glory*. The *Bema* judgement places a whole new complexion on this saying because it will

---

[532] 2 Corinthians 5:10
[533] Romans 14:10
[534] 1 Corinthians 3:10-13
[535] 1 Corinthians 6:12, 10:23

settle the degree of *promotion* earned during our earthly service, which we will enjoy in the everlasting life to come. We should see our lives as qualifying us to work for the Lord in some capacity in the Millennium, rather than expecting to merely sit on clouds playing harps![536] We will be judged as to how *faithful* we have been with the resources, gifts and responsibilities entrusted to us. It is not a question of how dramatic or high-profile our service has been, but how faithfully we have carried it out. Such service is likely to relate mainly to family, church, ministry and workplace settings. We all long for the Lord to commend us for having been that good and faithful servant. This first judgement will take place after Jesus comes for His Bride, the body of believers. It will be a judgement of the raptured saints and the resurrected dead in Christ.

Secondly, we come to the *judgement of the nations*, or the *sheep and goats* judgement.[537] Of the three ultimate judgements of God, this one is the most relevant to Israel, and yet also the most mysterious. This may be a judgement of the survivors from the Gentile nations – those who have come to faith after the Rapture. James teaches us, "faith, if it has no works, is dead."[538] According to this theory, true faith would be evidenced by how these individuals treated the *brethren* of Jesus, the suffering Jewish people in their time of greatest need.

Another view of the *sheep and goats* judgement sees it simply as a sifting process to separate those nations which supported Israel in her gravest trial, and those nations which hardened their hearts against her plight. This theory gives scope for the unsaved survivors among the *sheep* nations to enter the 1,000

---

[536] Matthew 25:14-30
[537] Matthew 25:31-46
[538] James 2:17

years, and may fit better with Zechariah's prophecy, "Thus says the LORD of hosts, 'In those days ten men from all the nations will grasp the garment of a Jew, saying, "Let us go with you, for we have heard that God is with you.""" [539] Such a tender verse also indicates a deep spiritual hunger in the Millennium.

It is generally believed, however, that it will only be those Gentiles with saving faith who come through the *sheep and goats* judgement to enter the millennial kingdom in their mortal bodies. [540] They are the blessed of the Father who will inherit a kingdom specially prepared for them since the foundation of the earth. Despite this, we know that ultimately unsaved descendants of those who enter the Millennium will be stirred up when Satan is unchained at the end of the 1,000 years to approach Israel for the second war of *Gog and Magog*. [541]

Whichever view of the passage is correct, it clearly confirms the distress of Israel in the *Time of Jacob's Trouble*. Jewish people will be hungry, thirsty, displaced, unwell, and imprisoned. In addition to nourishment, clothing, hospitality, medical care and compassion, support will also be required for them to travel to the land of Israel after the tribulation. "Thus says the Lord GOD, "Behold, I will lift up My hand to the nations and set up My standard to the peoples; and they will bring your sons in their bosom, and your daughters will be carried on their shoulders."" [542] "Surely the coastlands will wait

[539] Zechariah 8:23
[540] gotquestions.org "Who Will Occupy the Millennial Kingdom."
[541] Revelation 20:7-9
[542] Isaiah 49:22

for Me; and the ships of Tarshish will come first, to bring your sons from afar, their silver and their gold with them...”[543]

To understand this judgement, it helps to read the parallel description in Joel, which foretells “the sun and moon grow dark and the stars lose their brightness.”[544] The nations will be gathered into judgement on account of Israel, whom they have scattered and abused.[545] The people being judged are later described by Joel as the *surrounding nations* who will be gathered in the Valley of *Jehoshaphat*,[546] which translates as *God has judged*. This passage in Joel suggests that *all the nations* subject to the *sheep and goats* judgement will (initially, at least) be the *surrounding* nations that have had the most opportunity to help end-times Jewish refugees and captives.[547]

The amount of space in the Valley of Jehoshaphat is noteworthy. It is part of the Kidron valley, and it leads down to the Dead Sea and is less than a mile wide. Its best-known section is between the Temple Mount and the Mount of Olives. Over the centuries, some have commented on the problem of fitting the entire world’s population into this confined space. We can assume that this valley will be drastically changed when the Mount of Olives splits in two. The judgement may take place in waves, starting with the *surrounding nations*, gradually followed by groups from other nations further afield.[548]

The third judgement, the *Great White Throne Judgement*, occurs after the 1,000 years.[549] This is a judgement for those who

---

[543] Isaiah 60:9 See also Isaiah 14:2,
[544] Joel 3:15
[545] Joel 3:2-7
[546] Joel 3:12
[547] Matthew 25:34,46
[548] Luke 17:34-36
[549] Revelation 20:11-15

died without saving faith in Christ. They will be brought back to life for this. "And the sea gave up the dead which were in it, and death and Hades gave up the dead which were in them."[550] We read of the dead *standing* before God. These spiritually dead people sadly are those who will awaken to "disgrace and everlasting contempt."[551]

| Jehoshaphat | *Yehoshafat* | יְהוֹשָׁפָט |

[550] Revelation 20:13
[551] Daniel 12:2

18: The Millennium

"Then I saw thrones, and they sat on them, and judgment was given to them. And I saw the souls of those who had been beheaded because of their testimony of Jesus and because of the word of God, and those who had not worshiped the beast or his image, and had not received the mark on their forehead and on their hand; and they came to life and reigned with Christ for a thousand years." (Revelation 20:4)

We love to sing hymns and songs about heaven, and to marvel in our hearts as to what eternity will be like when the New Jerusalem fully descends to earth.[552] We can only wonder, since we lack the ability to fully understand what is ahead. The Apostle Paul hints at this mystery when he alludes to the book of Isaiah when writing, "THINGS WHICH EYE HAS NOT SEEN AND EAR HAS NOT HEARD, AND WHICH HAVE NOT ENTERED THE HEART OF MAN, ALL THAT GOD HAS PREPARED FOR THOSE WHO LOVE HIM."[553] We know that in the eternal state all people will have an everlasting resurrected body, that there will be no more unbelievers living, and that death will cease. As John writes, "Behold, the tabernacle of God is among men, and He will dwell among them, and they shall be His people, and God Himself will be among them, and He will wipe away every tear from their eyes; and there will no longer be any death; there will no longer be any mourning, or crying, or pain; the first things have passed away."[554]

By contrast, the Bible paints a detailed picture of the immediate future following the return of the Lord Jesus. In Revelation Chapter 20, the period of 1,000 years is mentioned six

[552] Revelation 21:2
[553] 1 Corinthians 2:9; Isaiah 64:4
[554] Revelation 21:3-4

times. This repetition indicates that we are talking about a literal period of time. We find a wealth of detail about the nature of the Millennium in the Old Testament. Understanding the doctrine of the Millennium brings into sharp focus many passages of the Hebrew prophets, which may initially puzzle some of us. Isaiah wrote that all the nations will flow up to Jerusalem, "Come, let us go up to the mountain of the LORD, to the house of the God of Jacob; that He may teach us concerning His ways." Weapons of war will become redundant; they will yet be refashioned into farming implements.[555]

There will be two sorts of people in the Millennium: those with a spiritual body like that of the resurrected Lord Jesus and those with a natural body like Adam's.[556] Believers who are raptured or resurrected at the Second Coming will be given "an imperishable body" and will "bear the image of the heavenly" body of the Saviour. "Just as we have borne the image of the earthy, we will also bear the image of the heavenly." By contrast, saved survivors of the final week of Daniel will enter the Millennium in their Adamic bodies.

The number of survivors will be few. We are told that following the time of the Lord's wrath, He will "make mortal man scarcer than pure gold."[557] We see that, like the aftermath of the flood in the time of Noah, there will only be a relatively small number of people left to repopulate the earth at the start of the Millennium. However, the world's population will grow rapidly during the 1,000 years due to the earth's idyllic conditions and the great ages to which people will live. The usual lifespan will be so much longer that dying aged one hundred

---

[555] Isaiah 2:2-4; Jeremiah 3:17
[556] 1 Corinthians 15:35-49
[557] Isaiah 13:9-13; Isaiah 24:6

will be regarded as a divine judgement and not as something to be celebrated, as it is now.[558] If man's lifespan returns anywhere near to that enjoyed prior to the flood, when Adam lived to be 930 years and Methuselah to be 969, then death would be a comparatively rare occurrence![559]

During the Millennium, Jerusalem will be called by a special name "The LORD is our righteousness.[560] Amazingly, the temple will be rebuilt yet again. Biblical commentators refer to this fourth temple as *Ezekiel's Temple*. The detailed description recorded by Ezekiel will serve as a blueprint for Israel to build the millennial temple. This accords with the plans King David was given by the Spirit for the original temple construction, "All this," said David, "the LORD made me understand in writing by His hand upon me, all the details of this pattern."[561] Ezekiel is similarly told to record the vision and all its details, "so that they may observe its whole design and all its statutes and do them."[562] It will be roughly one mile on each side,[563] which is too large to fit on the present Temple Mount site, but we know that there will be massive topographical changes following the great end-times earthquake.[564] New rivers and water fountains will appear: "I will open rivers on the bare heights and springs in the midst of the valleys; I will make the wilderness a pool of water and the dry land fountains of water."[565]

---

[558] Isaiah 65:20-23
[559] Genesis 5:5,27
[560] Jeremiah 33:16
[561] I Chronicles 28:12,19
[562] Ezekiel 43:11
[563] Ezekiel 42:15-20; 40-43
[564] Isaiah 40:4; Zechariah 14:10; Jeremiah 31:38-39
[565] Isaiah 41:18

Even the waters of the Dead Sea will one day be healed so that fish will thrive.[566]

Isaiah describes the Millennium as a time when the animal kingdom will be at peace, "the wolf and the lamb will graze together, and the lion will eat straw like the ox...they will do no evil or harm in all My holy mountain."[567] God's Holy Mountain refers to the New Jerusalem, where Jesus will reside with His saints in their immortal bodies. It may hover above, or be near to, the earthly millennial Jerusalem. It may even be that we resurrected saints will happily live among peaceable animals in the New Jerusalem!

Ezekiel explains to us that animals will be slaughtered as temple sacrifices in the rebuilt temple, which will be in the earthly millennial Jerusalem. In his vision, he is shown tables where the animals for the burnt, sin and guilt offerings will be killed and prepared for sacrifice.[568] Israel will once again honour God through temple offerings.[569] We may like to think of the whole population of the millennial earth being vegetarian, as Adam and Eve were before the fall. However, Ezekiel reminds these future temple priests that they may eat the sin and guilt offerings, but not any fowl or animal that either died naturally or was killed by other animals.[570] Ezekiel speaks of a sheep being offered "from each flock of two hundred" and we may therefore conclude that these creatures are not merely being nurtured for burnt offerings and wool. Likewise, the Passover will continue to be celebrated during the millennial period, and the killing and eating of the Passover lamb is part of

---

[566] Ezekiel 47:10
[567] Isaiah 65:25, 11:6-9
[568] Ezekiel 40:38-43, 43:18-27
[569] Ezekiel 43:27, 44:11, 45:17
[570] Ezekiel 44:29-31

that festival.[571] The fishermen will spread out their nets at En Gedi on the shores of the Dead Sea, and we can assume that this is because the fish will continue to be eaten as normal, since they are not used in the temple sacrificial system.[572]

Amos beautifully depicts the bountiful millennial harvests to come, when the time of reaping will last for so many months that it will overlap with the time for the following year's ploughing.[573] Zechariah paints a lovely picture of elderly people sitting in the streets of Jerusalem, while children play peacefully. He writes how those who survive from the nations which came against Israel will be required to commemorate the Feast of Tabernacles (*Succoth*, Booths) in an annual pilgrimage to Jerusalem. God will even withhold rain from any disobedient nation that flouts this requirement.[574] A nation which refuses to serve Israel "will be utterly ruined."[575] The former enemies of Israel will show them profound honour and respect.[576]

Israel will be honoured in the eyes of the world with a very special role in the Millennium. "Thus says the LORD, "The products of Egypt and the merchandise of Cush and the Sabeans, men of stature, will come over to you and will be yours; they will walk behind you, they will come over in chains and will bow down to you; they will make supplication to you: 'Surely, God is with you, and there is none else, no other

---

[571] Ezekiel 45:21
[572] Isaiah 41:18-20; Ezekiel 47:8-10
[573] Amos 9:13
[574] Zechariah 8:4-5, 14:16-21
[575] Isaiah 60:12
[576] Isaiah 60:14

God.""""[577] After the days of Noah, God again judged humanity; this time by dividing their languages as a punishment for their collective arrogance in building the Tower of Babel.[578] Whilst we know that the nations will retain their identity during the Millennium, we simply do not have details about specific languages.[579] God says, "For then I will give to the peoples purified lips," which can also be translated as *language* or *speech*.[580] This may suggest that the whole world will yet speak Hebrew, in a reversal of the Tower of Babel judgement. We know that God performs miracles for people's speech, such as when the pilgrims to Jerusalem heard the apostles speaking in their own language on the Day of Pentecost.[581] This is not beyond the realms of possibility during the Millennium.

Jerusalem will become a place of rejoicing rather than weeping. God promises, "for, behold, I create Jerusalem for rejoicing and her people for gladness. I will also rejoice in Jerusalem and be glad in My people."[582] It will be a joyful city with young couples celebrating marriage and a place of praise and worship at the temple. There will be "the voice of joy and the voice of gladness, the voice of the bridegroom, and the voice of the bride."[583] This must be describing the earthly Jerusalem during the Millennium since there is no marriage in heaven! In his prophecy, Joel poetically describes how "the mountains will drip with sweet wine and the hills will flow with milk."[584]

---

[577] Isaiah 45:14
[578] Genesis 10
[579] Isaiah 2:4
[580] Zephaniah 3:9
[581] Acts 2:6
[582] Isaiah 65:17-19
[583] Jeremiah 33:11
[584] Joel 3:18

The thousand years will see the fulfillment of the prophecy that Jesus will rule the nations with a rod of iron.[585] The saints will live in their glorious resurrected bodies in the New Jerusalem, from where they will rule and reign over the millennial kingdom with Him.[586] It will form part of that wonderful time referred to in Daniel 7:18, "But the saints of the Highest One will receive the kingdom and possess the kingdom forever, for all ages to come." The millennial earthly government of our Saviour and Lord is central to God's future plans for this world: "... an administration suitable to the fulness of the times, *that is*, the summing up of all things in Christ, things in the heavens and things upon the earth."[587]

Imagine a world not only with no war, but also an absence of government-sanctioned abortion and euthanasia. A world where there is no more famine nor pestilence. This is the kingdom for which we pray in the Lord's prayer, "Your kingdom come."[588] It brings fresh meaning to Jesus' Sermon on the Mount, which says that the meek will inherit *the earth*. Unlike the earthly Jerusalem where Ezekiel's temple will be in operation, the New Jerusalem does not need a temple, "for the Lord God the Almighty and the Lamb are its temple."[589] Founder of the International House of Prayer and Bible teacher Mike Bickle presents a persuasive view that the New Jerusalem will descend twice: coming down first to hover near to the earth

---

[585] Revelation 12:5
[586] Revelation 5:9-10
[587] Ephesians 1:10
[588] Matthew 6:10
[589] Revelation 21:22

during the Millennium and descending fully to the earth at the end of the thousand years.[590]

We may have personal or family prophecies which have not yet come to pass. Mike Bickle also makes the fascinating point that some of these will have their ultimate fulfillment in the Millennium. He alludes to personal prophecies made to Old Testament characters which are yet to be fulfilled.[591] Promises made to the likes of Abraham, Jacob and David were never realised during their earthly lifetimes.[592]

During the time of the thousand years, Yeshua, the Lion of the Tribe of Judah, will ensure that Israel will no longer be oppressed by her neighbours. She will be the head of the nations. "The LORD will make you the head and not the tail, and you only shall be above, and you will not be underneath."[593] The Millennium will be the long-awaited time when the announcement made to Mary by the angel Gabriel will finally come to pass, "and He will reign over the house of Jacob forever, and His kingdom will have no end."[594]

| Jerusalem | *Yerushalayim* | יְרוּשָׁלַיִם |

---

[590] Mike Bickle online library "Seven Reasons Why I Believe the New Jerusalem will be Near the Earth in the Millennium"

[591] IHOP Overview of Eternal Rewards, session 5 "Reigning on Earth in the Age to Come"

[592] Genesis 15:18-21; 28:13,14, 2 Samuel 7:12-16

[593] Deuteronomy 28:13

[594] Luke 1:33

Thoughts on Isaiah 40

It is my contention that the deeper one understands God's plan for Israel in the End Times, the clearer the Bible becomes. To illustrate this, I am referring to Isaiah 40, which I memorised as a young Christian – as I shared in my testimony at the beginning of this book. Whilst I never understood it all at the time, now I can recognise more of its true meaning.

You may like to turn to this passage of Scripture and imagine Israel after the harrowing years of the *Time of Jacob's Trouble*. We read of her deep need of comfort in the first two verses. Perhaps now we can more fully sympathise with the deep distress of Jerusalem's traumatised and bereaved survivors. Israel will have been humbled by God in a manner hitherto unthinkable.

We read of the Second Coming of the omnipotent Lord Jesus, "Behold, the Lord GOD will come with might, with His arm ruling for Him. Behold, His compensation is with Him, and His reward before Him."[595] Massive topographical changes will make way for the King of Glory, "Clear the way for the LORD in the wilderness; make straight in the desert a highway for our God. Let every valley be lifted up, and every mountain and hill be made low; and let the uneven ground become a plain, and the rugged terrain a broad valley."[596] Wicked end-times leaders will be swiftly judged: "He it is who reduces rulers to nothing, who makes the judges of the earth meaningless. Scarcely have they been planted, scarcely have they been sown, scarcely has their stock taken

---

[595] Isaiah 40:10
[596] Isaiah 40:3-4

root in the earth, but He merely blows on them, and they wither, and the storm carries them away like stubble."[597]

The future proclamation of the good news or Gospel (*Besorah* in Hebrew) of the Messiah will start at Jerusalem and then spread out to the other parts of Israel, "Get yourself up on a high mountain, O Zion, bearer of good news, lift up your voice mightily, O Jerusalem, bearer of good news; lift it up, do not fear. Say to the cities of Judah, "Here is your God!""[598] Israel is assured of the Lord's compassion and gentleness as He leads her forward to the Millennium, "Like a shepherd He will tend His flock, in His arm He will gather the lambs and carry them in His bosom..."[599]

The *Time of Jacob's Trouble* will be the culmination of Israel's millennia of fierce affliction. For a deeper perspective on suffering, we must turn to the book of Job. There we read that, as his ordeal was finally ending, the Lord emphasised His omniscience and wisdom to Job.[600] "Where were you when I laid the foundation of the earth? Tell Me, if you have understanding."[601] In Isaiah 40, Israel is likewise given a divine lesson on the greatness of God and the imponderable wisdom of His ways. "Who has directed the Spirit of the LORD, or as His counselor has informed Him?" and "... Have you not understood from the foundations of the earth? It is He who sits above the circle of the earth, and its inhabitants are like grasshoppers..."[602]

---

[597] Isaiah 40:23-24
[598] Isaiah 40:9
[599] Isaiah 40:11
[600] Job 38-41
[601] Job 38:4
[602] Isaiah 40:13,21-22

Israel is gently chided for reasoning that God had forgotten about her during the *Time of Jacob's Trouble*, "Why do you say, O Jacob, and assert, O Israel, "My way is hidden from the LORD, and the justice due me escapes the notice of my God."[603] This again finds a parallel in the account of Job, who complained against God, "I will say to God, 'Do not condemn me; let me know why You contend with me."[604] Like Israel in the future, Job was also rebuked for his musings, "Will the faultfinder contend with the Almighty?"[605]

God graciously restored Job after his terrible trial, lavishing upon him even more abundant blessings than at first.[606] Israel too is yet to enjoy yet richer blessings from the Lord than she has ever known before, "He gives strength to the weary, and to him who lacks might He increases power. Though youths grow weary and tired, and vigorous young men stumble badly, yet those who wait for the LORD will gain new strength; they will mount up with wings like eagles, they will run and not get tired, they will walk and not become weary."[607]

May Israel's end-times friends be more considerate and supportive than Job's comforters were to him, and may we all increasingly be blessed as we reread even familiar eschatological passages in the Word of God!

Good News	*besorah*	בְּשׂוֹרָה

---

603 Isaiah 40:27
604 Job 10:2
605 Job 40:2
606 Job 42
607 Isaiah 40:29-31

Chart of Chronology of Relevant History

Approx dates	What happened?	Bible reference
2000 BC	Covenant with Abraham	Genesis 12
1940 BC	Abraham takes Isaac to Mount Moriah, where the temple is later built	Genesis 22
1875 BC	Jacob and family move to **Egypt**	Genesis 46
1446 BC	Israel leaves **Egypt**	Exodus 13-18
966 BC	Solomon builds the temple in Jerusalem	2 Chronicles 3
760 BC	Jonah sent to Nineveh, capital of **Assyria**	Jonah 1-4
744-612 BC	**Assyrian** empire at its peak but does not include Jerusalem	Approx. time of Zephaniah
733-722 BC	Initial deportations by **Assyria** followed by capture of Israelite capital at Samaria	2 Kings 17
730-725 BC	Isaiah prophesies Child to be born and also judgement on **Assyria**	Isaiah 9-10, approx. time of Micah
612 BC	**Assyrian** empire overthrown by **Babylon** at Battle of Nineveh	
606-539 BC	**Babylonian** empire	
606 BC	First invasion of Judah by **Babylon**; Daniel and friends taken in deportation	2 Kings 24, Daniel 1:1
586 BC	King Nebuchadnezzar of **Babylon** destroys Jerusalem and temple	2 Kings 25, Jeremiah 52
585 BC	Ezekiel prophesies about Gog and Magog	Ezekiel 38-39
539-330 BC	**Medo-Persian** empire	Book of Esther
537 BC	Proclamation of Cyrus releases Jews from 70-year captivity and authorises rebuilding of the temple	Ezra 1
445 BC	Proclamation of Artaxerxes to rebuild Jerusalem	Nehemiah 2:1-8
430 BC	Malachi prophesies	Book of Malachi
331 BC	Alexander the Great defeats Persian King Darius III in rapid expansion of **Macedonian/Greek** empire	Intertestamental period
323 BC	Alexander the Great dies aged 32, **Greek** empire splits among 4 families	
167 BC	Antiochus Epiphanes IV (ruler of Syria, one of the 4 divisions of **Greek** empire) captures Jerusalem, desecrates temple by offering pig to Zeus	Rebellion by Maccabees leads to feast of Hanukkah (John 10:22-23)
27 BC-476 AD	**Roman** empire	Luke 2:1-20, Acts 22:28
5 BC	Birth of Jesus the Messiah	
30 AD	Crucifixion and resurrection of Jesus	
1285-1918	**Turkish (Ottoman)** empire ends in defeat during First World War	
1923-1948	U.K. Mandate over Palestine	

Chart of Beast Empires

Daniel 2 Statue	Daniel 7:1-8 4 beasts	Daniel 8 Ram and goat	Revelation 13:1-10 Beast with 7 heads and 10 horns	Revelation 17:9-17 7 heads plus one
				1st fallen (Egypt)
				2nd fallen (Assyria)
Head of gold	Lion with eagle's wings		Mouth of a lion	3rd fallen (Babylon)
Chest and arms of silver	3 ribs of bear are kingdoms conquered in rise to power	Ram, one horn higher than other	Feet of a bear	4th fallen (Medo-Persia)
Belly and thighs of bronze	Leopard with wings, fast animal	Male goat; notable horn Alex Great. 4 divisions (horns) include Antiochus Epiphanes IV; Seleucid kingdom	Beast like a leopard	5th fallen (Greek)
				6th is at time of Revelation (Roman)
Legs of iron				7th not yet come (Ottoman)
Toes of iron and clay	Incomparable with any living creature, exceedingly savage and brutal	Antichrist (Antiochus was a type) depicted as a little horn, grows from 1 of 4 divisions	One head mortally wounded, wound heals, head revives	8th of the 7 (revived Ottoman Empire?)

Epilogue

My thoughts on the heart of the Lord Jesus regarding Israel and the future

My children, My heart is heavy
As My wayward chosen ones are drawn towards
their destiny.
I formed them for My glory, as a light to the
Gentiles
Yet they replaced Me with empty cisterns, with
worthless idols.
I will not forget My covenant with them, My be-
loved ones.
I cannot fail them nor forsake them.
I will bring them through fire, through deep
waters
To refine and to sanctify Myself in their midst
That they may look upon Me whom they pierced.
I long to be glorified in their assembly
To receive their praise
For them to bow down to Me.
Jerusalem will be taken, half the city will go
into captivity.
They will cast lots for My people, barter a boy for
a prostitute
And a girl for a bottle of wine.
See Me, coming from Edom, My garments
stained with blood
In My anger, in My fury, to punish those who
are destroying My people.
Yet I take no pleasure in the death of the
wicked.

By My blood I purchased those from every tribe
And tongue and people and nation.
Whoever believes in Me will not perish but have
everlasting life.
I invite you to feel My heart; to allow Me to melt
your heart of stone.
Intercede for the victims and for the oppressors
For the weak and for the strong
For the children, for the parents, for the old
For the captives and for the armies.
Give Me no rest until I establish Jerusalem as a
praise in the earth
Until ten men from the nations grab the robe of
a Jewish man
And say, we want to go with you because we
have heard that God is with you.
I am a light to lighten the Gentiles, and the
glory of My people Israel.

Further Resources

If you do not already use a whole Bible reading plan, I encourage you to follow one to take in the entire sweep of Scripture. Be like the Bereans, and examine what is written in this book, to check if these things are really so. Bear in mind what Joshua told Israel shortly before he died, "not one word of all the good words which the LORD your God spoke concerning you has failed; all have been fulfilled for you, not one of them has failed."[608]

As you read the Old Testament, look out for how Israel fared under each of the beast empires. Reflect on the suffering of Israel in their slavery in the land of Egypt. Notice how the Assyrians conquered Samaria, and how they brought other nations into the land to intermarry and weaken the national identity of Israel.[609] Consider how Daniel and his friends would have felt in Babylon, having been forcibly removed from the land of their birth to serve the king of the Babylonian beast empire. Read in the book of Lamentations how Jeremiah felt with Jerusalem overrun and emptied. Empathise with the misery of the Hebrew exiles as they were taunted by the Babylonians.[610] Study what it was like for Israel in the Medo-Persian empire as you read through the books of Esther and Nehemiah. When you read the Bible, you will not directly come across the Macedonian Greek Empire. It existed in the period between the Old and New Testaments. However, it is dealt

---

[608] Joshua 23:14
[609] 2 Kings 17
[610] Psalm 137

with prophetically by Daniel and also elsewhere.[611] John's Gospel refers to the Feast of Dedication.[612] We are, of course, familiar with the Roman Empire's treatment of the people and the land of Israel in the New Testament. If you want to read about the Turkish Ottoman Empire, this is extensively recorded in the annals of secular history.

Your reading of the New Testament will be enhanced as you bear in mind the prophetic calendar set out in Leviticus 23. The gospels cover the days of Passover, Unleavened Bread and First Fruits, but are silent on the Feast of Trumpets and the Day of Atonement. The book of Acts describes the fulfillment of Pentecost when the Holy Spirit was poured out. It also references *Yom Kippur* as "the fast" or "Day of Atonement" in the description of Paul's sea journey to Rome.[613] The Feast of Tabernacles is alluded to in John 1:14, which seven more literal Bible versions[614] translate using the word "tabernacled" or "tabernacle," instead of "dwelt" or "lived."

I recommend YouTube teaching videos and books[615] by Nelson Walters of the Last Days Overcomers ministry. These resources excel in equating current events with the prophetic Scriptures, and distinguishing Mystery Babylon from the Antichrist's Beast empire by explaining how the woman initially rides the beast, before it turns on her and destroys her. Of particular interest is the book "Daniel Unsealed" by Nelson Walters and Bob Brown.[616] This provides a far deeper study

---

[611] Ezekiel 26; Zechariah 9:1-8
[612] John 10:22
[613] Acts 2, 27:9-10
[614] Young's Literal Translation, Literal Emphasis Translation, Anderson NT, Haweis NT, Worrell NT, A Faithful Version, Mace NT.
[615] Revelation Deciphered (2016). Rapture Case Closed?(2017)
[616] Ready for Jesus Publications (Wilmington, NC, 2018)

into the details of the end-times beast empires than is possible in my introductory "Chart of Beast Empires." For readers interested in the link between the four horses in Revelation Chapter 6 and how they relate to those in Zechariah 1 and 6, I would recommend to you a powerful series of sermons on YouTube by Keith Malcomson of Limerick City Church, entitled "The Four Horses of the Apocalypse." Christine Darg has written a slender book, "Appointment in Petra,"[617] with some fascinating biblical insights about this place of refuge for Israel. If you want a deeper understanding of the roles of the Church and Israel in these last days, Reg Kelly's website is very insightful: www.mysteryofisrael.org. There is also a wealth of information and teaching about the End Times, Israel, world events and Bible prophecy on the website of Tony Pearce: www.lightforthelastdays.co.uk. He also regularly produces a detailed magazine, "Light for the Last Days." If you are interested in Islamic theories about the End Times, Samuel Shahid has written *The Last Trumpet*,[618] which compares Christian and Islamic Eschatology. You may also like to read Joel Richardson's book, *Mid-East Beast*.[619] If the geopolitical content of our studies has been of interest, visit the website of *Zion's Hope*, where David Rosenthal hosts helpful material. This includes teaching on Neom and a video, *The Nature of the Beast*. There are detailed talks on the End Times in the Mike Bickle online library, under the category of *End Times and Eternity*, such as on Zechariah, Hosea, the Battle for Jerusalem, and the Jewish

---

[617] 2020. Printed in Great Britain by Amazon
[618] Xulon Press, 2005
[619] WND Books, 2012

end-times prisoners.[620] For a Jewish perspective, the Orthodox Temple Institute's website is instructive and interesting.

As to other relevant books, Rose Publishing produce *Then and Now Bible Maps*[621] showing the ancient empires and how they relate to their equivalent modern-day cities and countries. The biography of Eliezer Ben-Yehuda, who revived the Hebrew language, *Tongue of the Prophets*[622] by Robert St. John, gives a good idea of what it was like for Jewish people living in Jerusalem during the time of the Ottoman Empire. The role of Egypt and Assyria in the future is detailed in the book by Tom Craig, *Living Fully for the Fulfillment of Isaiah 19: When Egypt, Assyria and Israel Will Become a Blessing in the Midst of the Earth.*[623] Janet Willis has written a fascinating book, *What on Earth is Heaven Like,*[624] about the New Jerusalem, the Millennium and eternity. *The Time of the End*[625] by Tim Warner will challenge you to consider the question of when the return of Jesus will occur. *The Feasts of the Lord*[626] by Kevin Howard and Marvin Rosenthal is a good read if you are interested in God's prophetic calendar, as revealed in Leviticus 23.

Try and follow the news pertaining to Israel and the surrounding areas. If you can subscribe to Amir Tsarfati's ministry of "Behold Israel," it will keep you updated as to the security and political situation in Israel. Keep an eye too upon Iran and Turkey, two of the main nations involved in Ezekiel's description of the invasion and represented by the ram and the

[620] mikebickle.org/category/End-Times-&-Eternity
[621] RW Research, Inc., 2008
[622] Wilshire Book Company, 1972
[623] Drawbaugh Publishing Group, 2014
[624] Khesed Publications, 2011
[625] CreateSpace Independent Publishing Platform, 2012. AIR. answersinrevelation.org
[626] Thomas Nelson Publishers, 1997

goat in Daniel 8. Follow the news on the shifting alliances of Saudi Arabia (the probable location of *Sheba* and *Dedan*) as she chooses between Iran and Israel. It is most important to watch and pray for the United States of America, as discussed in Chapter 9.

The ministry of the late Derek Prince covered the distinctive nature of praying for Israel. His teaching is available in various formats including YouTube videos and a dedicated website.[627] For detailed prayer requests concerning Israel and the Jewish people worldwide, "One for Israel" produce a prayer guide. Many of you may already be subscribed to the prayer materials issued by "Prayer for Israel." U.K. Jewish outreach missions like "Messianic Testimony" and "International Mission to Jewish People," besides American ministries with a U.K. presence such as "Jews for Jesus" and "Chosen People's Ministry," produce regular newsletters and magazines. Individual missionaries involved in Jewish evangelism offer their own prayer letters. There is an excellent discussion about the tragic abortion situation within Israel on YouTube, "Putting an End to the Number One Cause of Death in Israel," produced by Tree of Life Ministries Israel.

If you have any questions or comments on these studies, please contact me via my family's website. The address is: www.fresholivepress.com. It also gives full details of my companion book, written to encourage those in the churches with a heart for Israel. "Hebrew Lessons for Beginners from the New Testament" offers easily understandable lessons for reading Hebrew, together with simple insights into the Hebraic background of the New Testament writings. Additionally, on

---

[627] Derek Prince Ministries

the website are some sermons with a Jewish background from my husband Robert, and a selection of his evangelistic tracts written for Jewish people. After decades of door-to-door outreach to Jewish people in London and Essex, at the time of writing, he is producing a series of special tracts for rabbis, Jewish leaders and celebrities, which he posts out to them. My late mother-in-law wrote her sad and moving life story in a 56-page booklet, "The Last Letter." This includes her account of living under Nazi occupation in Vienna and her subsequent escape via the Kindertransport rescue scheme. This is also available on request. Additionally, there is a section on the website featuring original Christian poetry. Be on the lookout on our website for a book by my husband on the life and ministry of David Baron, a brilliant Hebrew Christian evangelist, preacher and author of the 19th and 20th centuries, with a great interest in Jewish evangelism. We also plan to produce a Messianic Haggadah and Guide to Passover.

Index of Prayer Points

Hebrew Lessons for Beginners from the New Testament

Rosamund Weissman

This is written for Christians who want to learn Hebrew and who desire to deepen their understanding of the Hebraic background of the New Testament. This teaching is humbly offered to contribute towards "the equipping of the saints for the work of ministry, for the edifying of the body of Christ."

The New Testament contains a treasury of Hebrew thoughts and truths, thinly concealed beneath the so-familiar text. These gems are presented and examined through the medium of 12 beginners' Hebrew lessons. Each lesson can be approached in one of two ways. They are suitable for those who wish to learn or revise beginner's Hebrew. Alternatively, the English text can be read and appreciated in its own right (making use of the transliterations), without studying the Hebrew reading component. Whether you are reading this book to build up your knowledge of Biblical or modern Hebrew, or to inspire you in poetry, song, or craft activities, may you be blessed!

Available via fresholivepress.com